Queer Mythologies
The Original Stageplays of Pam Gems

By Dimple Godiwala

Pam Gems: 'I have such reverence for writers who are true explorers, who break form and content, who have that generosity which breeds vitality.'

Queer Mythologies
The Original Stageplays of Pam Gems

By Dimple Godiwala

intellect
Bristol, UK
Portland, OR, USA

This book is for Rohan, Natasha, Taira and Gina to help them
appreciate a part of their cultural heritage
—
With love

First Published in the UK in 2006 by
Intellect Books, PO Box 862, Bristol BS99 1DE, UK

First Published in the USA in 2006 by
Intellect Books, ISBS, 920 NE 58th Ave. Suite 300, Portland, Oregon
97213-3786, USA

A catalogue record for this book is available from the British Library

Image of Pam Gems © Clive Barda Tel: 020 87410805 Fax: 020 8563 0538

Cover Design: Gabriel Solomons
Copy Editor: Holly Spradling
Typesetting: Mac Style, Nafferton, E. Yorkshire

ISBN 1-84150-135-2

Printed and bound in Great Britain by 4edge Ltd.

CONTENTS

FOREWORD BY PROFESSOR TIM PRENTKI

Tim Prentki is Professor of Theatre for Development at University College Winchester and co-author of *Popular Theatre in Political Culture* (Intellect 2000). He is presently preparing a monograph on the Fool as agent of social transformation in European theatre.

Dr. Dimple Godiwala has expertly undertaken the first comprehensive appraisal of the theatrical oeuvre of Pam Gems at a moment when her profound influence on the development of English drama is in danger of being seriously underestimated through critical neglect. Besides offering vital insights to the individual plays, Dr. Godiwala has succeeded in linking them to a coherent internal development within the life and work of Pam Gems. She is assisted in this task by access to Ms Gems and her son for insights into the contexts in which much of the work was created. Most importantly, she never loses sight of a particular play as a performance text and so is able to capture the theatrical essence in ways that transcend any literary achievement. This capacity is especially important in any analysis of Pam Gems' achievement since it is predicated upon a fierce desire to work against the grain of the theatrical establishment. Godiwala captures this anti-establishment motif that runs through the plays through her own development of a definition of queer theory which is used ingeniously and effectively to forge connections and to demonstrate the gradual unfolding of Gems' preoccupation with the outsider and the misrepresented. Yet at the heart of Gems' strategy of defiance lurks a paradoxical desire to be let into the limelight which many of the protagonists exhibit. This desire is implicitly linked to Gems' own situation: at once a scathing critic of the mainstream, yet simultaneously penetrating it to effect irrevocable changes to it. Central characters like Queen Christina and Edith Piaf who make their worlds on their own terms are nevertheless depicted as being at the mercy or rather the agency of those by whose permission they are allowed to appear in their starring roles. Though hungry for performance, they still cling tenaciously to an identity which defies the expectations of their audiences, even as Gems in her handling of their characters lures the audience towards a love/hate relationship to them. Godiwala reveals with clarity and penetrating insight, the ways in which this paradox is indicative of the attitudes that Pam Gems herself experienced in relation to the English theatrical establishment; at times enjoying the spotlight of the main stage and critical acclaim but more often suffering the consequences of a refusal to compromise her artistic vision.

This volume marks a significant contribution to the rehabilitation of Pam Gems' reputation, and Dr. Godiwala reveals herself as a major critical voice on the contemporary literary and theatrical scene. This monograph is an absolute necessity for any students of Gems' work and an important extension of applied critical theory in performance.

Tim Prentki
University College Winchester 2005

ACKNOWLEDGEMENTS

For a semester's sabbatical which enabled me to complete this book, I thank the School of Arts at York St John College. For commissioning the book and funding the writing, a big thank-you to Jonathan Gems. I am also immensely grateful to Jonathan Gems for providing appendix and other material, acknowledgements are elsewhere in this text. I am grateful to Pam Gems for making many of the still unpublished playscripts available. I owe gratitude to Professor Vincent Gillespie (Lady Margaret Hall, Oxford), Jonathan Gems, Emeritus Professor Peter Thomson (University of Exeter), the anonymous reader at Intellect and most especially Professor Tim Prentki (University College, Winchester) and Stephen Michael McGowan who gave generously of their time to read the manuscript and advise.

I am grateful to Alan Sinfield for his original and stimulating point of view and Jon Stallworthy for being always challenging and inspiring.

I would also like to acknowledge my colleagues for the many discussions which have helped with my writing over the years, particularly Suzanne Stern-Gillet, Bill Luckin, Makiko Minow-Pinkney, David Rudd, Brid Andrews, Harold Robinson and David Richmond.

For the help they extended, my thanks to all the librarians and staff at York St John College Fountains Learning Centre, in particular, Lottie Alexander, Anthony Chalcraft, Claire McCluskey, Adriana Lombari, Fiona Ware and Linda West. I am also grateful to Grant Saker at York St John for typing the appendix.

My thanks to all at Intellect Books who helped make this book possible, especially my editor May Yao and, for her careful copy-editing and helpful comments on the text, Holly Spradling.

For her regular long-distance support and constant good cheer I would like to voice my appreciative thanks to my sister Falguni Mather, and for the sumptuous meals out whenever they are in town, my thanks to her husband David. I am ever in the debt of my husband Stephen Michael McGowan for his support, encouragement, appreciation, abundant love and understanding.

I am grateful to Heidi Burns at Peter Lang, New York, for granting me permission to use the material on Pam Gems from my previous book, *Breaking the Bounds: British Feminist Dramatists Writing in the Mainstream since c. 1980* (New York: 2003).

A revised version of the section on *Aunt Mary* was published in Gender Queeries (Gender Forum), Number 8, 2004. This article was first read as a paper at the July 2004 University of Manchester Conference "Queer Politics and Cultural Production" which was dedicated to the work of Professor Alan Sinfield.

INTRODUCTION

A dramatist as prolific and talented as Pam Gems ought not to need an introduction. Her plays have been celebrated feminist additions to English drama in the Long Twentieth Century.[1] In *Breaking the Bounds: British Feminist Dramatists Writing in the Mainstream since c. 1980*, I briefly introduced the work of Pam Gems. Cannily on the pulse of the cultural moment, she proves it time and again in her work. It was once said of Marina Warner that she was able to spot cultural pre-occupations before they became part of the cultural *zeitgeist*. Gems' dramaturgy anticipates many such cultural moments, later institutionalized and reified by prolific academic theorizing on the subject/s. It is important to note the time of writing of many of the plays: *Queen Christina* (produced in 1977) was written before Hélène Cixous plausibly and philosophically theorized about bisexuality, and can be said to be Gems' prefigurative dramaturgical answer to Cixous' lament about theatre in 1977:

> It is always necessary for a woman to die in order for the play to begin. Only when she has disappeared can the curtain go up; she is relegated to repression, to the grave, to the asylum, oblivion and silence. When she does make an appearance, she is doomed, ostracized or in the waiting room. She is loved only when absent or abused, a phantom or a fascinating abyss. [...] That is why I stopped going to the theatre; it was going to my own funeral, and it does not produce a living woman or (and this is no accident) her body or even her unconscious.[2]

Aunt Mary, first produced in 1982, prefigures by more than a decade the prolific output on 'queer' theorizing in the Anglophone world. The triad seems to be an appropriate answer to the destructive potential of the nuclear family as theorized by Deleuze in the 1970s (*Anti-Oedipus*).

Oedipus is the figurehead of imperialism, "colonization pursued by other means, it is the interior colony, and we shall see that even at home … it is our intimate colonial education." […] Oedipus is everywhere.[3]

THE THESIS

Gems' white mythologies are *herstories* but also histories which, contesting the *logos* and *mythos* of male reason, are populated with characters who challenge the stereotypes of western culture. Jacques Derrida speaks of white man's mythology:

> Metaphysics – the white mythology which reassembles and reflects the culture of the West: the white man takes his own mythology, Indo-European mythology, his own logos, that is, the mythos of his idiom, for the universal form of that he must still wish to call Reason. *Which does not go uncontested.*[4]

Derrida is talking about the Indo-European heritage he culls his concepts from as one that is kept logical as he bends it to the limit of Reason that has dominated western philosophy.[5] This Western universal – white mythology – can be compared to the patriarchal tradition that British drama has constructed itself in: a lineage which was seldom contested until the onset of feminist, race and other issues in mainstream drama as I theorize in *Breaking the Bounds*. It was Pam Gems who once averred: 'I am at war … with the principal personage of traditional philosophy, that abstract subject who masquerades as everyone and anyone, but is really a male subject in disguise.' In this book, I demonstrate that Pam Gems, in contesting the *logos* and *mythos* of male reason, creates a mythology of the O/other to contest the white male dramaturgical hold on centuries of British drama. Significantly, she challenges the domination of *white man* as she brings in the O/other. Not only is Woman cast as the Other, Freud's dark continent of otherness, but other cultures, eastern and western are brought into play with characters from 'home' (England). The normative heterosexuality of European man too is shattered by portraying him as coloured by all the shades of his beingness: straight, gay, transgendered, bisexual. Perhaps it is not surprising that the part-gypsy, working-class Gems' mythology in being inclusive of all minoritarian others can be classed as 'queer' as Alan Sinfield's reading has it.[6] Contesting mainstream tradition, Alan Sinfield contends that 'simply to set aside mainstream culture would be to leave much of its power unchallenged.' In a conceptual phrase which extends further the fluidity of gay and lesbian sexuality indicated by Judith Butler in *Gender Trouble*, Sinfield's readings of 'class, ethnicity, gender and sexuality' transmute queer from merely 'homosexual' into subcultural theory. Thus *queer mythologies are those of gender, class, race, ethnicity and sexuality which challenge the status quo of the dominant white middleclass mainstream.* Gems writes in these very subcultural spaces to give us a drama which entertains as well as educates, in the best tradition of English drama, even as she brings in *difference*.

These are the queer mythologies which severally contest the white patriarchal traditions of British drama, carving out, for Gems, an authorial identity which, overspilling the gendered space that the twentieth-century British feminist dramatists locate themselves in, becomes subsumed in the queer ex-centric spaces of minoritarian identities and sub-cultures.

GEMS AND HOLLYWOOD

Gems' popularity as a playwright produced often in the West End and her widespread appeal can be linked to her plays being on the pulse of cultural iconology. An impassioned cinema-goer in her youth, Gems' morphologies are often constructed like quick film cuts. As she puts it in her foreword to *Marlene*, she belonged to what 'was the first generation – in the twenties – to grow up with the movies as an integral part of life.'[7] Hollywood figures large in her memories of influences, and reveals itself in the re-presentation of Garbo and Dietrich. Disrupting the linear realist narrativization of classical cinema, Gems re-writes Dietrich and Garbo for the stage in non-chronological time-shifting non-linear cinematic form.

Early feminist film theory (1970s and 1980s) was largely an attempted critique of Hollywood cinema. Theorists, obsessed by the psychoanalytic insights of Freud and Lacan which were fashionable in the early days of Anglophone theory even though their phallogocentric bases wrote out the possibility for women's subjectivity, equality, agency or choice, predictably functioned in a contradictory way when it looked at woman, especially female stars, in Hollywood film. Denying the subject position of woman (and here she is decidedly the white middle-class woman as early feminist theorists completely elided the subjectivities of race, class and gay sexuality) and defining her, after psychoanalytic theory, as a site of lack or negativity and an absence, the feminist film critic was able to see herself, through an identification with the female stars, only masochistically and as an object of male desire. The cult of the female star in Hollywood was not for a long time linked to notions of women's fantasy identifications and a source of pleasure (as it undoubtedly must have been for the critics), but, seeing through male eyes, as psychoanalysis allowed only a male subject, critics such as Laura Mulvey, followed by E. Ann Kaplan et al, spoke (in feminist terms and never acknowledging the Sartrean source) of the *male* gaze, the pleasure of the male spectator and the function of the distinctly male mechanisms of voyeurism and fetishism which constructed the female subject as a reassuring phallic object through the man's controlling gaze and desire. Functioning within and controlled by the Law of the Father, these early feminist critics theorized by means of a binary logic, a technology of thought that French feminists such as Cixous had already revealed as phallocentric. Producing, as Mulvey does, notions of identity which are oppositional and a result of what Deleuze and Parnet call 'the binary machine', a technology that produces and distributes rigid roles pretending to universality, the film critics of the 1970s and 1980s reproduced the very structures they purported to critique. Rodowick's detailed critique of Mulvey's 'Visual Pleasure and Narrative Cinema' interestingly reveals that Freud's schematization of male and female is much more ambivalent, diffused and differentiated than Mulvey's rigid phallogocentric logic.[8] However, Freud's contention that there is only one libido, masculine, and that the castration complex and phallic envy are to be observed in children of both sexes leads to the binary analyses of Mulvey et al which posits the male in the centre of their theories. Femininity by psychoanalysis's technology of definition, is always passive and masochistic, which leads the feminist film critics to theorize the female spectator to be so.[9]

Although, of course, these early pioneers of feminist film criticism in the Anglophone world do make several insightful discoveries about Hollywood cinema, revealing its heteronormative bias and its maintenance of the status quo of the white western world, they seldom reflect that these cinematic representations follow from western society's uneven and hierarchical nature and therefore film is *a posteriori* the ideology of the West.[10] It is not film nor the film-maker who produces these structures; they are always already embedded in societal structures prior to their encoding in film, or indeed drama, art, literature, music. If Hollywood had not afforded these female critics pleasure, they would not know it intimately. Ironically, feminist film critics, whilst seldom admitting that Hollywood films afforded them pleasure, when they do accept 'the magic of Hollywood [and] its skilled and satisfying manipulation of visual pleasure' they masochistically speak of women acquiring pleasure *in the act of being regarded as objects of the male gaze*. Speaking of Hollywood as a 'dream factory producing an oppressive cultural product'[11] these early theorists never acknowledge how or why they knew Hollywood so well. They envision, without really hitting upon an alternative, cinema which would come 'from leaving the past behind without simply rejecting it, transcending outworn or oppressive forms, and daring to break with normal pleasurable expectations in order to conceive a new language of desire'.[12] What a non-normative pleasure or a new language of desire might look like is never voiced.

Acknowledging both pleasure and desire, Pam Gems speaks of early identification with the stars both male and female.[13] Almost as if she were directly confronting the phallogocentric contradictions and race and class exclusions the feminist film critics found themselves practicing, Gems' plays written since the early 1970s construct the woman not only as *subject* but one possessing *agency* (e.g., *Queen Christina* 1977), acknowledge a range of sexualities and gendered positions (*Aunt Mary* 1982, *Queen Christina*), construct complex inter-racial subjects (*Go West, Young Woman* 1975, *Deborah's Daughter* 1992), all of which no Anglo-American white middle-class feminist theorist was able to conceptualize till the 1980s. Moreover, Gems constructs woman as subject who 'owns the gaze' in E. Ann Kaplan's phrase; and she does this in several ways: firstly, by destroying their to-be-looked-at ness, especially when she is reworking the myths played by the stars Garbo and Dietrich: Christina's entrance is the best example, and so is casting the ageing Siân Phillips as Marlene in the play of the same name. Secondly, by destroying the conceptualization of the roles played by female stars such as Dietrich and Garbo, which portrayed woman as an enigma and a mystery (e.g., Lola spits in her mascara, making herself up in front of her suitor). And thirdly, by making her characters metaphors for the shifting and contradictory identities of contemporary women in destroying the psychoanalytic notion of woman as eternal and unchanging.

Pam Gems' female characters possess agency as self-determining subjects and are constructed to allow the female spectator recognition, identification and pleasure. Indeed, the agency of the authorial subject, framed as she has been by the male tradition of British drama, is evident in the choice of subject/s, in the production of a variously gendered meaning, and in the construction of an alternative morphology. If writing, like film-making, demonstrates unconscious processes at work in the authorial subject, the result, in the gamut of Gems' work, is a distinctly *different* consciousness. Transforming the language of the patriarchal unconscious, Gems' female characters, whether historical, mythological, Hollywood icons or ordinary women, function as signifiers to allow a female audience identification with a signified which symbolizes 'contemporary identity'. Here, it is *woman* who is 'reassured' as she is seen as a figure of autonomy and independence; a subject who owns and controls her desires. This is the barely voiced, scarcely formulated alternative the Anglo-American theorists sought for in vain in film and Cixous lamented the lack of in drama.

It may be said that drama, by its very nature of staged reality, possesses the quality of self- consciousness that film, (theorized to be constructed in imitation of the (white western) patriarchal unconscious or, elsewhere, a fantasy dream screen that (masochistically) pleasures the white middle-class woman and gratifies and reassures white man), does not. However, if the history and legacy of western film is a patriarchal one, then the bounds of the centuries-old discourse that frames Gems' dramaturgy especially in the early days of the 1970s – the English drama – is also one which has been dominated and constructed by the male point of view. Pam Gems' brilliance and originality as a dramatist rests in the fact that she could conceive subjects of difference in a period – the 1970s – which few white middle-class Anglo-American feminist theorists thought to write about (until it became politically correct or fashionable to do so), whilst simultaneously offering her female spectator *pleasure*, (conceived of mainly masochistically by our early psychoanalytic Hollywood watchers), and in subversive forms, disruptive in the production of normative meanings a decade or so before white western woman formulated her theories and arguments for the ever-shifting, plural subject positions of gender and sexuality; long before she was forced to include the racialized subject in her theorizing; indeed long before the white western feminist theorist was able to see her self as an autonomous *subject*, of pleasure, of agency, of desire.[14]

Disrupting the patriarchal modes of both classical Hollywood cinema as well as the English male dramatic tradition she is circumscribed by, her characters are metaphors for contemporary women and men. She often *herstoricizes*, thus righting the balance of dramatic history by creating central parts for women in British drama.

Pam Gems' commitment to feminism goes beyond the writing of the plays. She founded the Women's Theatre Group in 1971, the first theatre company organized by women to produce plays written by women, and was involved in setting up the first-ever season of plays by women at the Almost Free Theatre under director Ed Berman. The deliberate writing of central parts for women to add to the limited canon of central parts for women thereby creating the opportunity for actresses to become stars (via starring roles) conferred power on women within the malestream.

The importance of Gems' early recognition of some of the most important issues of the feminist twentieth century to rupture heteronormative western patriarchal constructions of literary and dramaturgical meaning make her drama even more performable on the politically correct stages of today. With reference to feminist and cultural theory, this book aims to contextualise Gems' dramaturgy within the Long Twentieth Century's feminist concern with severally dismantling, as well as its attempt at restructuring, the concepts which formulate the normative consciousness of the western world, and particularly, British society. These concepts range from inter-sexual and inter-racial relationships to straight and alternative identity formation, making this book a critique of Gems' several queer readings, which is one way of conceptualizing her writing. Like most serious feminist writers, Pam Gems' plays are not superficial pieces which skim the surface of things. They are about deep issues which concern us all – race and difference, art and the artist's responsibility, history, psychology and psychoanalysis, and most importantly to feminists, women's ever-shifting identity in contemporary Britain.

This book is an attempt to critically situate Gems' original stageplays within the mainstream. As such, it excludes her numerous adaptations of European plays (by European playwrights) for the stage, which are listed in the appendix. Although her adaptations also speak for her remarkable subversiveness, it is in her original scripts that she displays the marked breaking of bounds in a series of queer performativities which characterizes the best of her work for British theatre.

NOTES

1. The Long Twentieth Century extends the twentieth century into the present day, continuing the influences of the late twentieth century in terms of ideas, style and form. See my book, Breaking the Bounds: British Feminist Dramatists Writing in the Mainstream since c. 1980 for the multiple transgressions wrought by feminist dramatists on patriarchally inherited forms and styles.
2. Hélène Cixous, 'Aller à la mer' (1977), in Richard Drain (ed.), Twentieth Century Theatre: A Sourcebook, London and New York: Routledge, 1995, p.133.
3. Gilles Deleuze and Félix Guattari, Anti-Oedipus: Capitalism and Schizophrenia Vol. I, [1972], trans. Robert Hurley and Mark Seem and Helen R. Lane, Athlone Press, 1984, p.xx.
4. Jacques Derrida, 'White Mythology' (1971), in Margins of Philosophy, trans. Alan Bass, Chicago: Chicago University Press, 1982, p.213. Emphases mine, except for the Greek words which are italicized in the original.
5. Western reason does not transcend its own bounds as does logic in Indian philosophy. Western thought does not, even in Derrida, break the bounds of reading and writing. See Dimple Godiwala and William S. Haney II's 'Editorial: Derrida's Indian Philosophical Subtext', Consciousness, Literature and the Arts, Volume 5, Number 2, August 2004. http://www.aber.ac.uk/tfts/journal [Archive].
6. See Alan Sinfield, Cultural Politics: Queer Reading, University of Pennsylvania Press, 1994, p.ix, pp.66–67; Alan Sinfield, The Wilde Century: Effeminacy, Oscar Wilde and the Queer Moment, Columbia University Press, 1994.
7. Pam Gems, Introduction to *Marlene*, Oberon books, 1998, pp.7–9.
8. See David N. Rodowick, 'The Difficulty of Difference', in E. Ann Kaplan, Feminism and Film, Oxford University Press, 2000, pp.181–202.
9. See David Macey, Lacan in Contexts, Verso, 1988, pp.177–178.
10. Although Claire Johnston does acknowledge as much in her 1973 essay, it is seldom picked up

on by subsequent critics. Another critic who notes this is Elizabeth Cowie, 1978. See 'Women's Cinema as Counter-Cinema'; 'Woman as Sign'. In E. Ann Kaplan, (ed.) Feminism and Film, Oxford University Press, 2000.

11. Claire Johnston, 'Women's Cinema as Counter-Cinema', p.23.

12. Laura Mulvey, 'Visual Pleasure and Narrative Cinema', in E. Ann Kaplan (ed.) Feminism and Film, Oxford University Press, 2000.

13. Pam Gems, Introduction to Marlene, Oberon books, 1998, pp.7–9.

14. For seminal essays on feminist film theory written in the 1970s and 1980s, See Claire Johnston, 'Woman's Cinema as Counter-Cinema', 1973; Laura Mulvey, 'Visual Pleasure and Narrative Cinema', 1975; Elizabeth Cowie, 'Woman as Sign', 1978; Mary Ann Doane, 'Woman's Stake: Filming the Female Body', 1981; E. Ann Kaplan, 'Is the Gaze Male?' 1983; Gaylyn Studlar, 'Masochism and the Perverse Pleasures of the Cinema', 1984; Miriam Hansen, 'Pleasure, Ambivalence, Identification: Valentino and Female Spectatorship', 1986. In E. Ann Kaplan, Feminism and Film, Oxford University Press, 2000. Additionally, see the theories of Julia Kristeva, Judith Butler.

1

BEGINNINGS

Born in Bransgrove, Hampshire to a poor working class family in 1925, Pam Gems started to write drama at school at the age of six or seven. During the war years and after she wrote four television plays for the BBC which never saw the light of day, she wrote a few plays for the radio with little success. In the 1950s one television play, *A Builder by Trade*, was accepted for television. Although this play portrayed working-class relationships, 'they did it very middleclass [although] I wanted it to be about working class people and nobody seemed to know what I was talking about.'[1]

Betty's Wonderful Christmas was Gems' first produced play in 1972. Produced at the Cockpit Theatre in London, the producer was David Aukin who later became co-director of the Royal National Theatre, head of Channel Four Films, and a successful West End producer. *Betty's Wonderful Christmas* was directed by his wife Nancy Meckler, renowned for many theatre and film productions and for her work with Shared Experience Theatre Company. Set in the early 1920s, the play has autobiographical overtones in the class setting and childhood of meagre possessions. Naturalism dominates the stage directions: 'A man sells hot potatoes. They are real, and so is the smell.' (p.7) However, this is not a naturalistic play. Jonathan Gems describes it as 'a Jungian-feminist dream play, heavy with symbols of the animus, the anima, and changelings from the dark pools of the collective unconscious. It may also owe something to the work of child psychologist Bruno Bettelheim, and, formalistically, to the verse dramas of the 19th century which gave us plays such as Ibsen's *Peer Gynt* and informed the Victorian tradition of pantomime.'[2]

In her early plays Gems focuses on poverty in the lives of young women and how they cope and survive. The two short monologues, *My Warren* and *After Birthday*, as well as *Ladybird, Ladybird* are likewise influenced by the deep naturalism of the 'slice-of-life' school of western drama. The difference is that they are about women of the lower middle and working classes. It would be too easy for critics to dichotomize Eileen of *My Warren* and Lindsay of *After Birthday* as spinster and abusive mother, but as Gems reminds us in her preface, they are both survivors, 'trapped in social time [...] they are not simply objects of social concern, which would be to patronise them.' That Eileen, the stereotypical lonely spinster, sent a vibrator as a joke, is able to derive sexual satisfaction from using it sends her out of the strictly demarcated space that forms the stereotype. Lindsay who has killed her unwanted child ends up in prison. As Gems puts it, 'the nature of her survival may not be orthodox or particularly convenient for society.' Equally, Eileen is not 'a "frigid spinster". Such a woman does not exist.'[3]

Ladybird, Ladybird is grimly naturalistic in its detail of a working-class mother whose younger children have been taken away by the social services and put in care. The play satirizes the system and also reveals the precarious position of a young widow with several children. The grim detail of the dirty house, the unkempt mother and the hungry children is offset by the officious and insensitive social worker to whom they are just another 'case' on the files. Betty of *Betty's Wonderful Christmas* is also a survivor like the female protagonists of the early plays. As the pantomime drama diverges into fantasy she meets a prince and later is offered to be taken in by a wealthy lady. Betty rejects both and chooses her mother and her home.

Gems' plays have a deep grammar even as she keeps with traditional form in her early work, yet she has often been mistaken for a dramatist who is just a 'fun' writer. As Gems herself puts it, 'I have such a reverence for writers who are true explorers, who break form and content ...' yet, she adds, 'When I pay for my ticket and go through the door, I want to be engaged, to be filled with life.'[4]

Pam Gems 'went to a church school, then [won a scholarship to Brockenhurst] grammar school, a very good school where they read operas in French'.[5] She later joined the WRENS. After the war she went to Manchester University. At University she wanted to read English but when she went to sign up for courses, 'the queue was three times around the block' and she decided to 'find a very short queue' and ended up reading psychology for her first degree where she studied Jung, Adler, Sigmund Freud, Anna Freud, among others as well as being embroiled in the existentialism craze which was raging at the time and which included, thanks to the work of Simone de Beauvoir and others, fierce debates about the nature of female-ness and the integration of female principles and qualities into the patriarchal matrix of society. Pam Gems was part of the first post-war generation which was doing the thinking which provided the intellectual climate necessary for the social revolution of the 1960s and 1970s. A number of her plays stem from this experience and the interests it sustained. In 1976, Lala, her youngest child, a Down's syndrome baby, went to school and Pam Gems had more time to write. She wrote *Dead Fish* later called *Dusa, Fish, Stas and Vi*.[6] Pam Gems believes in the social-contractual nature of marriage and is against the idea of abortion as well as single mothers rearing children. Having married once, she has four children. Her husband, Keith Gems, an architect and wax model manufacturer whose family firm, Gems Wax Models (est. 1885) has supplied wax figures to Madame Tussauds, made the first British fibreglass mannequins, 'Fashion Sketch' designed by Adel Rootstein who had worked in Keith Gems' wig department. Pam Gems also designed a couple of mannequin ranges.[7] In the existentialist 1950s the Gems lived in Paris for a while, and later moved to London from the Isle of Wight.[8] Pam has been a gardener and worked for the BBC.

Gems' experience spans three generations – the war, early inclusive second-wave feminism, and the later separationist third moment (late 1970s and 1980s) which heralded a death knell for popular feminism. Gems' non-separationist integrated approach to gender speaks for her early political commitment.[9] Her essay 'Imagination and Gender' echoes Cixous and reflects on the need for gendered writing: '[You can't] write other than from yourself. If you're a woman you're bound to write as a woman'.[10]

Perhaps it is because Gems did not write seriously for the theatre until her forties that her feminist consciousness emerged onto the British stage with a mature mixture of empathy and distance. Possibly, too, it is this mix that allowed her to make the transition from the fringe, where her work first appeared, to the established theatres where her plays have been so frequently produced.[11]

She is the only feminist dramatist in the mainstream who, despite being imbricated within the dominant heterosexual matrix, has consistently reflected on normative and regulatory ideals such as heterosexuality; and specifically, reflected on the construction of women's sexuality in the forced matrix of subcultural and exclusionary Other: the prostitute. Despite her feminist political commitment, Gems is the only woman dramatist to have been produced by the Royal Shakespeare Company five times: *Queen Christina* (1977), *The Danton Affair* (1986) and *The Blue Angel* (1991); *Camille* and *Piaf* and then *Marlene* on London's West End in 1997.[12] Her gender-based thinking is conditioned by the early 1970s inclusive approach to class, race, colour; grass-roots feminism for every woman.[13]

> Today's chemically mutated woman has been released from the murderous dangers of traditional childbed. We are able to begin to explore, to become aware of ourselves autonomously, to be on our own feet, and to write – and rewrite our own history. We have to discover who and what we are. We must discern our own needs, our demands [...] And of course a woman writer cannot but be involved in this vital and exciting and profound movement. Being allowed in, being asked to join is one thing. But we are half the world, and this demands proper accommodation.[14]

Gems is careful to distinguish between political polemic and subversion as a function of drama; in her work subversion becomes the means and the end of dramatic writing as she undercuts mythology, heterosexism and 'woman' thereby subverting the dominant ideology.

> I think the phrase 'feminist writer' is absolutely meaningless because it implies polemic, and polemic is about changing things in a direct political way. Drama is subversive.[15]

Gems did not initially see herself as a feminist writer for reasons perhaps similar to her metaphoric construct, Queen Christina, who failed to understand the blue-stockings' open hostility to men, and the separate non-integrated lives they chose to lead. Gems' subject matter is gender-based as a direct result of feeling the need to right the balance and give women a voice and presence on the masculine formulated stage; the need to see woman as centre-stage in a collective solidarity which never implies a hostility between the sexes.

> The antagonism between the sexes has been painful, an indictment of our age. It is true that many women have been drawn, properly, to the Women's Movement after abuse by bad husbands, fathers ... they have had hopes pushed aside, seeing brothers favoured from infancy. It makes for grievances, fear and resentment. But, as often, one sees men hopelessly damaged by women [...] their mothers. *We cannot separate ourselves.*[16]

In this articulation of her belief that men as well as women are both victims as well as perpetrators of the system, caught up within it, inexorably damaged and damaging, she echoes a post-structuralist perspective. Surprisingly, for a dramatist whose central roles are undeniably for women, she [has] 'sometimes wondered why there hasn't been more backlash, militant groups formed by men, in retaliation [to feminism]'.[17] 'There will always be the chauvinists among us, *of both sexes* …'[18] '[but] if we believe that there is only Us, then something is released, something egalitarian …'[19] Gems seems to believe in a kind of bi-sexuality in which both genders can merge and contribute toward an integrity and ethics in identity formation; a bi-sexuality which is a construction by an integration of genders: an 'Us' which is reflected in the characterization of Christina's bi-sexuality as metaphor.

Although Gems' central characters are women, it has not been her purpose to alienate them from interacting with men. Her integrationist approach seems separate from her almost *her*storical writing, until we realise that her almost non-controversial stance to the history of drama (which has been undeniably male) emanates from the belief that writing is a gendered phenomenon. If the lineage of English drama is male it is because the writers have all been male. This may seem (almost) simple as an approach but when read in conjunction with her texts, this belief emerges as a supportive structure for writing which is always female/feminist and on the side of women, penned, undeniably, by a woman for women. She endeavours, moreover, to delineate women as a category within which lie limitless possibilities. She (re) discovers; she un-thinks the unifying regulatory history which seeks to homogenize and categorize a multiplicity of voices and gendered positions under the single rubric, 'Woman'. She is Cixous' woman writing woman.

NOTES

1. Pam Gems in an interview with Michelene Wandor, *Spare Rib*, September 1977, p. 12. This is an interesting fact as Gems' characterization of the working classes predates the fascination that class difference provided to mainstream theatre-goers in the 1950s.

2. 'In a phone interview with Pam Gems, she recalled that the play came about because producer David Aukin asked her to write a "Christmas play". She remembered that because the play was for children (as well as adults) and that children are "dry sponges hungry for water" she put in lots of information. One of her two most vivid memories of the first production was a gratifying moment when Yvonne Antrobus, the actress playing Betty, after having been told all the absurd requirements she had to fulfil in order to be accepted at the royal palace, and worried that she had forgotten them, asks herself rhetorically what they are. At this, many school children in the audience put up their hands and yelled: "Please Miss! Please Miss!" Yvonne Antrobus stopped and asked the children what she had to remember –

and they told her every single detail! The second moment Pam Gems remembered with pleasure was at a performance where the 7 year-old son of actor Charlie Hanson was in the audience. One of the parts played by Charlie Hanson was that of the Dragon, and, at the point where the Dragon (in pantomime style) is being booed loudly by the audience, this little boy ran on to the stage shouting at the audience to shut up because it wasn't really a dragon – it was his dad!' As quoted in a letter to the author from Jonathan Gems, 18 April 2004.

3. Preface to *My Warren* and *After Birthday*.

4. Pam Gems, 'Imagination and Gender', in *On Gender and Writing*, ed. Michelene Wandor, Pandora Press, 1983, p.150.

5. Pam Gems in an interview with the author, 8 May 2001.

6. Pam Gems in an interview with the author, 8 May 2001. Letter to the author from Jonathan Gems, 18 April 2004.

7. For information on Keith Gems, see http://www.ucl.ac.uk/~ucbtdag/bioethics/Keith.html and http://www.geocities.com/FashionAvenue/1122/mannequin_gallery/gemini/

8. Pauline Peters, *The Sunday Times*, 3 February 1980.

9. For an early critical appraisal and biography of Gems, see Michelene Wandor, *Carry On, Understudies*, Routledge and Kegan Paul, 1981, 1986, pp.161–166.

10. Pam Gems, 'Imagination and Gender', in Michelene Wandor, ed., *On Gender and Writing*, Pandora Press, 1983, p.148.

11. Katherine H. Burkman, 'The Plays of Pam Gems: Personal/ Political/ Personal', in *British and Irish Drama since 1960*, ed., James Acheson, The Macmillan Press, 1993, p.191.

12. The other RSC dramatist is Timberlake Wertenbaker, but her plays are adaptations and re-workings of Greek classics. Gems manages to bring feminism directly to the mainstream with subversive intent.

13. This early feminist consciousness which celebrated difference by including women of race, class and colour is reflected in the now defunct 1970s feminist journal 'Spare Rib'.

14. 'Imagination and Gender', p.149.

15. Interview with Ann McFerran in *Time Out*, 21–27 October 1977, as quoted in *Carry On*, p.162.

16. Pam Gems, in an afterword to *Dusa, Fish, Stas and Vi*, in *Plays by Women: Volume 1*, ed., Michelene Wandor, Methuen, 1983. My emphasis.

17. 'Imagination and Gender', p.150.

18. 'Imagination and Gender', p.150. My emphasis.

19. Gems in *Plays by Women: Volume Five*, ed., Mary Remnant, Methuen, 1986, p.48.

2

White Women's Mythologies

Gems [snatches] back the truth about women's lives out of the jaws of a male-constructed history. – *Mary Remnant, quoted in Rage and Reason*

A woman's (re)discovery of herself can only signify the possibility [...] of never being simply one. It is a sort of universe in expansion for which no limits could be fixed ... – *Luce Irigaray, 'This Sex which is not One'*

Woman un-thinks the unifying, regulating history that homogenizes and channels forces, herding contradictions into a single battlefield. – *Hélène Cixous, 'The Laugh of the Medusa'*

Western woman is a queer category.[1] Having been elided from the British stage in terms of the production of drama, today's Woman is not a singular category but a plurality and a diversity. In fact, it is not 'women's experience' itself but thinking from a contradictory position, that produces feminist knowledge.[2] Gems' plays chart the possibility of a radical plurality of voices within specific categories of gender and sexuality, voices which speak from the contradictory positions of bisexuality (*Queen Christina* and *Marlene*), whoredom (*Camille, Piaf*, Stas, Lola), and the feminine/feminist split (*Loving Women*). The dramaturgical re-workings of the films starring Dietrich and Garbo (*Queen Christina, Marlene, The Blue Angel*) establish that feminist stagecraft can disrupt the normative assumptions of cinema whilst offering pleasure and identification for the contemporary female spectator.

THE HISTORICAL WOMEN

Gems often writes woman-as-history. From Queen Christina's search for identity, to Guinevere's declaration of equality and Pasionaria's socialist and feminist work, Gems' women are a product of their time and yet transcend temporality to become ringing metaphors for contemporary womanhood.

Identity Politics: Queen Christina

I love the storm and fear the calm.[3]

Bisexuality unsettles certainties: straight, gay, lesbian. It has affinities with all of these, and is delimited by none. It is, then, an identity that is also not an identity, a sign of the certainty of ambiguity, the stability of instability, a category that defines and defeats categorizations.[4]

Within the category of woman-as-queer, Hélène Cixous endorses an 'other bisexuality' which is multiple, variable and ever changing, an excess which arises out of a 'non-exclusion either of the difference or of one sex'. Thus, characteristic of this 'other bisexuality' is a storm of differences which are stirred up, pursued and thereby increased. Thus *l'écriture féminine* 'will always surpass the discourse that regulates the phallic system'; it 'can never be theorized, enclosed, coded'. This 'dynamized' writing is constantly in exchange, a bisexual process which is 'infinitely dynamized by an incessant process of exchange from one subject to another'.[5] Queen Christina is intended by Gems to be a metaphor for the bisexual and constructed gender identity of contemporary woman. She is written as this Cixousian storm of excess, an overspill of dual-gendered sexuality who functions as mythical sign for contemporary fe-male sexuality. Both Fe(y) and Male, Fe/Male, this is *herstory* dramaturgically contemporized by Pam Gems.

In 1973, The Royal Court Theatre (run by Nicholas Wright and Bob Kydd) commissioned Pam Gems to write a play. When she finished and delivered *Queen Christina* in 1974, they turned down this radically subversive playtext – 'they said it was too sprawly, too expensive to do' and that '*it would appeal more to women*'. In an interview with 'Spare Rib', Gems said: 'That really got to me. I mean would they ever have said, 'We can't do this play, it will appeal to men?'[6] It made conventional English theatre history, however, as it was the first play scripted by a contemporary woman to be produced by the Royal Shakespeare Company in 1977.

Queen Christina is historiographic in its method and approach as are the later *Camille* and *Piaf*, *The Blue Angel* and the 1990s *Stanley* and *Marlene*. Gems undercuts mythologized figures in a Barthesian way, enabling a de-construction of the received notions which these icons are culturally imbricated within. These mythical morphologies are 'signs' within and of western culture, cultural artefacts that *is* Barthesian 'myth'. These can be defined as cultural significations which accrue on the linguistic sign, reducing the latter to a signifier which then functions alongside the cultural signified to form the associative function which postulates itself as a greater sign – a culturally specific, historically specific, constructed meaning which is *myth*. Myth functions as 'natural' meaning rather than artifice; it is naturalized in the psyche of the reception community rather than perceived as fictive.[7] Gems' focus on each myth destroys it – not, as in Barthes, by cynically making its intention obvious – but, by subversively deploying it to radical ends such as the de-construction of regulatory heterosexuality or hierarchical and dominant ideologies. This does not, as in Barthes, merely demystify or unmask, but gives it a sardonic twist which is 'allowed' onto the mainstream stages as it (the subject) is presented in the mystificatory *guise* of myth.[8] As Barthes notes, the worn-out state of each myth 'can be recognized by the arbitrariness of its signification'; just as 'the whole of Molière is seen in a doctor's ruff',[9] so all of Piaf-as-myth is signified on stage in the first strains of '*je ne regrette rien*'; but the contemporary re-presentation of gender-identity-as-construction, Christina-as-metaphor is unrecognizable as she lopes on stage as an unbecoming disabled fe/male. These myths, outworn as well as newly constructed, accrue significance as the play proceeds and become 'garrulous, a speech wholly at the service of the concept.'[10] Their meaning is distorted by the concept the dramatist is deploying each myth for; the dramatist-mythologist of gender allows a 'repetition of the concept [*e.g.*, compulsory heterosexuality] through different forms' allowing her audience 'to decipher the myth'. 'It is the insistence [of the concept] which reveals its intention.' 'But this distortion is not an obliteration' but, in fact, garrulous not merely with memory, but with *new, potentially deconstructive meaning*.[11]

Feminism is a movement which has theoretically influenced traditional disciplines, breaking, in its wake, the bounds of history. To historicize, for the feminist, would involve a re-search and a re-writing of traditional history to re-discover women where there exist records only of great men. This writing of the history of women is named herstory by separationists.[12] A few fringe dramatists and women's theatre groups have re-written historical as well as canonical drama since second-wave feminism began its task of consciousness-raising, but none in so sweeping and consistent a manner as Gems' de-construction of ideology via myth-breaking.[13] Herstorians do not concern themselves merely with 'political' figures, since the feminist endorsement of the personal as political, signifying the largely twentieth-century movement of women from the private domestic sphere of the home to the outer public sphere. Herstorian dramatists deconstruct patriarchal cultural ideologies operative in politicized private and public spaces. The feminist endorsement of the personal as political is the crux of feminism:

> Feminism is resoundingly political. One of the slogans that is perhaps most familiar is the claim that 'the personal is the political'. By this light, it seems, feminism refuses the gendered distinction of a male sphere of public life from a female realm of domestic economy. Feminism insists that politics is not something that happens between men alone: the supposedly natural order of relations between men and women is itself political, a matter for discussion and struggle. Even traditional notions of the nature of the political, which exclude or severely restrict female participation, have a gender politics.[14]

Indeed, feminism since the movement for suffrage has been deeply political. In feminist dramaturgy too, then, the political is imbricated in every decision. Bourgeois feminist critics such as Susan E. Bassnett-McGuire have criticized Gems 'for giving a single actor such a central role and for allowing her feminist heroine to become too embroiled in her personal problems.'[15] The fallaciousness of this argument is that whilst it privileges the collective over the individual (thus Bassnett-McGuire endorses the collective Magdalena Project whilst condemning Gems' individual authorship) it sets store in what is, finally, a masculinist negation of emotion and feelings. Seen from a broadly feminist viewpoint, the political significance in dramaturgical terms of a single strong female char-actor, such as Betty, Emma Weekes, Queen Christina, Piaf, Camille, Marlene, Mrs. Pat, Ebba and others, is an attempt to right the balance against a history of strong central male roles.

Gems skilfully creates forceful women whose contradictions and conflicts parallel the self-doubt of contemporary western woman. Her mythologies are metaphors for many a contemporary dilemma of gender. Moreover, she creates strong central male characters, such as the artist-figure Stanley Spencer, the intellectual boor Franz, Garibaldi and Nelson, revealing that her art and ideology embrace both genders.

The contemporary feminist search to understand the cultural nature of sex and gender identity subtexts much of Christina's dramaturgical character development. Diane Elam's summary of feminist positions on gender and sex is as follows: '... is "women" primarily a natural or a cultural category? The rough distinction between sex and gender can be made as follows: either sex is privileged as a biological attribute upon which a gender ideology is imposed, or sex is denied as merely the ideological mystification that obscures cultural facts about gender. [...] some feminists have argued that sex is not natural at all, that there is no natural identity behind the masks of gender, there are only the masks.'[16] Judith Butler's is the leading argument for the construction of sex. She argues that sex is a regulatory ideal which functions as a norm but is also a part of the regulatory practice that *produces* the bodies it governs. Sex is a reiterative and citational practice by which discourse produces the effect 'sex'.[17] I accept that sex is constructed inasfar as sexes are regarded as two, and anomalous cases are forced (by the medical profession which serves as the regulatory practice of society in bodies that matter, to use Butler's phrase) into occupying one or the other site. Certainly, as Butler has it, the performativity of gender is reiteration of a norm or a set of norms. It conceals or dissimulates the convention of which it is a repetition, making performativity a kind of citationality. Sex is imbricated within and formulated by discursive practices which compel the differentiated citations and approximations into binary sites called 'feminine' and 'masculine'. The production and articulation of sex is thus forced into *materialization* of a norm, constructing bodies that matter within the heterosexual matrix.[18]

The playtext of *Queen Christina* is Gems' attempt to portray the flux, uncertainty and instability which surrounds gender identity in postmodern culture. In a note prefacing the play, Gems explains: 'All plays are metaphors, and the dilemma of the real Christina, reared and educated as a man for the Swedish throne, and then asked to marry and breed for the succession, is perhaps not irrelevant today.' The playtext also offers a critique of western dualistic thought as it celebrates the interlinking of difference and identity. Although the ideal of unity of oppositions goes back to metaphysical foundations in western philosophy, contemporary post-Enlightenment thought is deconstructive as difference is understood to undermine the notion of stable identity; identity which is always in process, a *becoming* which is always in formation. Thus identity can never be stable nor natural as traditional western epistemology assumed it to be.[19] There is no *stable* subject: as Butler puts it, 'the "doer" is variably constructed in and through the deed.' Being constituted by discourse does not mean being determined by it nor does it imply that subjects are mired in 'culture' or 'discourse' The *supplément*, the excess of predicates which intersect to formulate feminist or gender identities is illimitable. Thus, there is no prediscursive 'I'.[20]

Queen Christina's body (sex) as well as gender refuse the conformity required of them, her privileged status perhaps activating a will to be produced differently. Perceiving male and female in terms of binary oppositions, (as western patriarchies do to make a forced classification of the sexes), leads us to a false position. It was originally Hegel's view that the laws of logic and the laws of nature are one, therefore difference should not be understood in the form of pure antinomies, of binary oppositions.[21] Diane Elam explains Hegelian dialectic as one which means 'that, within the thesis stands the difference of the antithesis, and vice versa. That is to say, neither thesis nor antithesis is purely identical to itself: within the 'I' there is always 'Not-I'.[22] Vis-à-vis Hegel, we read Christina to reject her female/ feminine biological sex (Not-I) which is simultaneous to the masculine gender she occupies at will, the 'I' of her gender/sex construction. It is Butler, however, who reveals the pitting of 'I' against an 'Other' as *a strategy of domination* particular to the western epistemological mode. 'Once [the] separation [between 'I' and 'Other'] is effected, [it] creates an artificial set of questions about the knowability and recoverability of that Other.[...] this binary opposition is a strategic move within a given set of signifying practices, one that establishes the 'I' in necessity, concealing the discursive apparatus by which the binary itself is constituted.' Thus the signifying practices of western epistemology conceal its own workings and naturalize its effects.[23] As Derrida puts it, '[W]hite mythology – metaphysics has erased within itself the fabulous scene that has produced it, the scene that nevertheless remains active and stirring, inscribed in white ink, an invisible design covered over in the palimpsest.' He calls this a 'dissymmetrical – false – dialogue' which is located on the *outside* of (male) western knowledge, it is the 'exergue' that 'does not deserve its position'.[24]

Within signification lies the 'agency' of epistemological discourse. The 'I' of discourse is both enabled as well as restricted by the *repetition* of regulatory ideals (the feminine, the masculine, heterosexual desire). The agency of the subject is limited within the orbit of compulsion to repeat; agency, then, is merely the possibility of *variation* on the repetition. Thus the formulation of Christina's identity can only lie within the practices of repetitive signification. Her variation of sex/ gender is based upon a citational performativity of an Other which is masculine/ male in its construction, repudiating all female/ feminine performative citations. This is a result of not being offered a choice; she has to live with the consequences of being trained to be a man in every way, but eventually expected to do her duty by the throne and produce an heir as queens are expected to do. Christina's sex and gender is forced into materialization whereby she demonstrates agency in repudiating wife/mother-hood.

The idea for the play came from the Garbo film: Gems had succumbed to the myth of Christina as a 'shining, pale, intellectual beauty' until her own research proved otherwise.[25] The Garbo film was made in 1932. Garbo herself was a 'lucrative and highly commodified product of MGM'. Although the Hollywood censors stressed the importance of avoiding any tinge of homoeroticism, the film addresses 'a wide range of sexual and gender positions outside permissible [...] heterosexual limits'.[26] Both Garbo and her performance as Queen Christina are carefully constructed images of a culture's myth-making. The off-screen Garbo's aloof and sphinx-like attributes conflate with the iconic Queen to mythologize her on-screen as Gems first perceived her: glamorous, enchanting, magical myth rather than the conflictual gender-transgressive masculine bisexual of Pam Gems' 1977 play.

In history, Christina has been documented as assuming the ceremonial functions of a monarch at the age of six, and as the French ambassador Chanut reportedly realized, 'she meant to run this country herself.' She took her first step toward wresting the initiative when she was only ten years of age, manipulating the Senate's choice of guardian to suit her own preferences. She insisted on being present at the Senate's deliberations on matters of State two years before she had attained full majority. In 1647, when she came of age, she declared, 'Now the fate of this country rests entirely upon my shoulders'. Betty Millan calls her 'the most intriguing of women and – above all – the most learned of queens.' Rather than a warrior-king, Christina was a philosopher-king. Typical of contemporaries' recorded perceptions of Queen Christina were: 'nought of a child except her age, nought of a woman except her sex' (Sforza Pallavicino); 'not like unto a woman, but courageous and wise (Chancellor Axel Oxenstierna, who headed the Council of Regency that ruled in Christina's minority); 'science are [sic] to her what needle and thread are to other women' (Madam de Motteville).[27]

Pam Gems' play opens with the reigning King's necessity to 'make a man of' the child Christina. The Queen has had several miscarriages, failing to produce the much needed heir, which provokes the King to declare that his only surviving child, a daughter, be prepared for the mantle of Kingship:

> King: We do have an heir.
> Axel: A girl.
> King: She's fit enough. Intelligent.
> Axel: But the wrong sex! With a weak succession it'll be anybody's game, we
>   can't have a woman.
> King: Make a man of her then.
> Axel: How?
> King: Training. [...] I want her fit, educated, able to lead an army if necessary. (I, i)

What we get is a 'Renaissance woman [who] hunts, fights, is bi-sexual and takes an active part in military and political decisions.'[28] Scene ii is an effective scene which incorporates a dramatic shock technique with humour, written to undercut the popular assumption of Christina as a pale shining beauty: 'Enter a German prince waiting to be received as suitor' to the now adult Queen Christina. Enter 'a beautiful young woman … wearing a simple but beautifully cut riding habit. Her pale ringlets fall about a beautiful but thoughtful face'. The prince, 'enchanted, moves forward, smiling with delight'. The young woman is followed closely by 'a battered figure in hunting clothes [who] appears to be slightly crippled, or perhaps it is that one of his shoulders is out of true, giving him a swivelled, crooked appearance'. The man's familiarity with the beautiful young girl, taken to be Christina, enrages the suitor who splutters: "I see I see! So this is our future consort … trailing a fellow about her like a common … a common … […] it is outrageous … bloody outrageous ….", as the 'man' (Christina) responds, thumping the prince genially on the shoulder, sending him reeling: "At least there's some spunk in him." (I, ii). The prince, alarmed, is totally unprepared (as is, one expects, the audience) for the man to reveal him/ her self as Queen Christina, who dismisses him as perfunctorily as she has done all the suitors shown her. Christina dresses, looks, behaves, and thinks like the man she has trained to be; she has fulfilled the monarchical need for a male heir; she has materialized the very morphology forced on her.

Christina's personality contains both sets of dichotomous elements with which the masculine sex has been stereotyped: she is a dashing man of action but also a reflective thinker. She is always questioning: war, life, Creation, Christianity, freedom are never taken for granted but subjected to constant debate and scrutiny. In Act I, scene iii she converses with René Descartes, the French philosopher and mathematician who provided a mechanistic basis for the philosophical theory of dualism. Although their conversations in the play never veer into abstract philosophical discussion, the implication, not unfounded, is that Christina has had the opportunity and the inclination for intellectual companionship. She was a prodigious reader and drawn to scholarship; she surrounded herself with scientists and philosophers; she was a patron of intellectuals. She has a healthy appetite for the pleasures of the body as well as the spirit, surrounding herself with beautiful young girls whose bodies she delights in, as they seem to serve as an alternative, more beautiful mirror for her own self which she views as ugly, a 'freak'. As she tells Ebba, 'by God, when I'm with you I forget, *you* become my mirror, I see *your* face, *your* eyes' (I, ii). She is equally not averse to the male, as long as he does not shower her with compliments to her physical beauty, the absence of which the queen mother has never ceased to remind her daughter of. Christina's view of her own physical appearance is honest if harsh, and when Karl professes his love she rebukes him: "Do you think I want to be desired by the likes of you? A man who fancies a long-nosed cripple? Since there's no sap of ambition in you, and I doubt you've the wit for contrivance, it must be aberration! [...] There's one freak on the throne ... no need to perpetuate the joke. The answer's no" (I, iii).

Christina, however, seems to possess a *jouissance* denied to her mother by patriarchal norms as the latter is forced into being a gendered societal construct of her time. The queen mother is paradigmatic of a biological reproductive machine whereas Christina is best described by utilising the Lacanian phrase – 'a *jouissance* beyond the phallus' quite literally – if only to signify her non-dependance on males for her pleasures. For Christina, "the prospect of a royal marriage is about as effective as a forced march through mud" (I, iv). As she observes:

> We live on sufferance. To your desires. I find you a cruel sex. [...] No man follows me. They follow symmetry, and all the thought in the world won't give me that. No, I'm damned if I'll breed for them. (I, iv)

Christina's querying, philosophical nature is evident from the opening of the playtext. War, violence, destruction are already being analysed and questioned by the learned queen as she is depicted in earnest dialogue with Ebba, whom she loves:

> Christina: Why are we given life? In order to suffer ... to be stoic? If so, why the larch tree? Why you? I think! To what purpose? For to believe we're here because ... or in order to – why that's to accept the most horrifying malignancy or the unbelievably inept! Pestilence ... the murder of children – by design? Better no meaning at all, I begin not to believe in anything ... oh, don't worry, I keep it to myself. (I, ii)

Christina is depicted as a blend of ideological and material doubt. In her, mind and body, abstract and physical, doubt and desire meet and blend to form an uneasy gender which, though it seems to combine the traditional oppositions, does not result in a desirable androgyny but, instead, an uneasy site of confused identity. There is no harmony in this uneasy meeting of male/female, only an intense dissatisfaction. Her strongly male gender identity combines with the refusal to marry and reproduce, as the latter is also a refusal to accept the limitations thrust upon her if she crosses the boundary of her constructed male gender.

> Axel: The beauties of both sexes that you see fit to keep about you are costing the privy purse a fortune.
> Christina: Oh come, a few wild oats, surely?

Axel:	So far as I'm concerned, once there's an heir, you can do as you please.
Christina:	I see. Tell me, how many royal confinements do you require before I'm allowed to fornicate? To secure this throne, give or take a miscarriage or so, will take the next twenty years of my life. If it doesn't put me under the ground.
Axel:	The same for all women.
Christina:	All the more reason to stay chaste.
	[...]
	Why didn't you leave me in the parlour with the rest of the women, it's what you want!
Axel:	Not at all. Your unique position demands both the manly qualities of a king, and the fecundity of a woman.
Christina:	Well, you can't have both.
Axel:	Why not? For twenty years I've prepared you for it.
Christina:	And how? By making a man of me. A man, despising women – just like you. You've had your joke, you and nature between you. (I, v)

Christina subverts the pressing political need for an heir in her denial of her biological female sex, but perhaps the real and more personal reason is confided to Ebba: "No man who wants a person?/ No such luck." (I, ii) Christina's existential dissatisfaction leads her to reject 'this cauldron of ice' where she is sure she will never find the answers she seeks. Although warned by Axel:

Axel:	They will not have the succession without the marriage. And if you continue to prate about choice, freedom, and all the other fashionable rubbish you'll have the Church at your throat and I shan't answer for your future, your throne or your personal safety. Have I made myself clear? (I, v)

she abdicates and makes for Rome and France, looking for stimulus of mind. Christina exhibited an antipathy to Lutheranism and converted to Catholicism. Historically, she abdicated after selecting her cousin Charles Augustus as her successor and heir. Three days after the abdication ceremony, dressed as a man called Count Dohna, she left for Rome. After a notorious life she died in Rome in 1689.[29] Act II dramatizes Christina's period of self-discovery and personal growth. Her encounter with the French blue-stockings leaves her unable to identify with their separationist lifestyle. Ironically, they have long admired Christina for her independent views and freedom-seeking ways, but it is a case of misplaced admiration. They do not realize that Christina *is* a man, and does not identify with their hatred of men. It is *women* Christina does not understand, in fact frequently despises, although she loves their bodies like a (heterosexual) man. In the forced materialization of her gender, Christina is more a male misogynist than a female separationist. The construction of her 'sex' is a product of the particular power relations that she is constituted within. She is a historically specific product, but more particularly, produced by the imperial powers which demand a *male* heir. Her 'sex' is thus an effect of power relations. Queen Christina is subject to a set of social norms – regulations – which determine her as male sexed. Her sex, gender, pleasures, desires are inevitably formulated in a binary site of opposition to female. However she overspills the site of male-ness in a bisexuality of desires, while she operates and functions within the framework of intelligibility enforced by one part of a binary relation. This puts our queen in some confusion and a need to resolve her gender amongst other freedoms she questions and demands.

From France and the blue-stockings to Rome, and Catholicism and the Pope offer our queen no answers either. Of course, she manages to shock Rome with her iconoclastic views which are pronounced 'blasphemous' by the Pope. Her bisexuality and libidinal excess surface in her dialogues with the Pope:

Pope: Confession connotes repentance.
Christina: Oh, I don't repent. Best time I ever had in my life … that's something we're going to have to put right in your religion. Celibacy's no good – not in the bible, you know. Think again … no need to cut it off, Pope!
(II, ii)

When Christina accepts the papal request to fight for Naples she is fully aware that the self-same Pope who denounced abortion as an act which "[turned woman] into an assassin" (II, ii), is now using her as a tool for the purpose of "Christian warfare". She accepts, however, more for the sake of her Neapolitan lover Monaldescho, than for Rome. It is in the course of this battle that she, in one sweeping violent motion, barbarically slaughters the traitor who was her lover.

Act II, scene vi reveals an emotional and reflective Christina repenting grievously for what she now recognizes as a brutal deed. If 'male' and 'female' were on a shifting continuum, where male occupied one end of the scale and female occupied the other end, this is where Christina's gender starts to slide from male to female. Taking place within her is the realization of the fact that she has been taught to *take* lives but born to *make* them. Close to the sights, smells and sounds of babies and women and domesticity, she heals and shifts up the continuum to being female. Living with

Lucia, for the first time she glimpses what her royal masculine heritage has denied her: "So warm down there! The smell of ironed clothes … linen … lace – Food … baking … And babies. The smell of babies. I like the smell of babies – can that be wrong? (II, vii).

The concluding scene is forceful in its implications on her (hypothetical) future: she rejects the papal offer of the Polish throne, and having saved a child's life – in an impulse opposite to the slaying of Monaldescho – she reflects on being a woman. She lashes out at Cardinal Azzolino, the papal ambassador:

> Yet who are the poorest of all? Women, children … the old. Are they the fighters, the creators of war? You say you want me for the fight, and, it's true, I was bred as a man, despising the weakness of women. I begin to question the favour. To be invited to join the killing, why, where's the advantage? Half the world rapes and destroys – must the women, the other half, join in?
> […]
> I begin to see that I have been a traitor to my sex – oh, I believed, when I commanded an army, that I fought for the weak and the helpless. […] I don't condemn every man as a murdering brute, far from it, or we'd not have survived so far. But when I think of it … young men destroyed, infants burned in their cradles … women violated … how wrong, how wrong I have been to condemn women for their weakness … they have kept us alive!
> […]
> Don't tell me what I can have if I fight. I won't fight. I won't fight, I tell you, I won't fight! If you want arms and legs to blow up, make them yourself. I want my children, do you hear … (II, vii)

Lynn Sukenik's term 'matrophobia' was defined by Adrienne Rich as 'the fear not of one's mother or of motherhood *but of becoming one's mother*'.[30] Christina's prolonged negation of marriage and motherhood can be traced to this fear. In identifying childbirth and the pain and difficulties attendant upon it with her mother, who had suffered fifteen years of painful miscarriages in a vain attempt to produce an heir; coupled with Christina's masculine training to take on her future role as 'king', Christina's matrophobia prevents her from desiring anything which would make her remotely resemble her long-suffering mother. At a time when the natural process of childbirth had not been eased by the progress of medical science, when women were compelled to produce heirs even if their biological systems were especially frail, the prospect of motherhood could be daunting. Rejecting the generation-based thinking which upheld motherhood as an example and an ideal for the daughter, Christina had transgressed into a bisexuality, throwing out ideas of marriage and motherhood which had seemed synonymous at first. It is only when she has renounced her kingdom and her throne, when bearing a child is no longer for purposes of State but realized as a personal want or need, that Christina's desire has space to grow. Christina, in reaching a state of self-actualization, repudiates war and violence. In repudiating the negative (masculine), *i.e.*, the futility in taking life, she is able to welcome the positive (feminine), *i.e.,* the ability to make life.

Pam Gems described the play as a 'uterine' play.[31] Christina's hysteria [Gk. *husterikós*, f. *hustéra* womb] is quite literal at the end of the play, and her final words to the departing cardinal are an unmistakable metaphor for the female-power she has finally come to terms with (apart from being a pun on her intellectual abilities): 'I am well'.

Christina's sexuality is an excess (a well) in the play of pleasures as she crosses from male to uterine-female. The insight about violence produces the effect of womb-identification. Her 'multiplicitous sexuality' flows and is reconfigured into the 'uterine' as her 'biological duplicity' comes 'into play'. Queen Christina, textualized, is a sign of unnatural transgression which, for her, becomes fatally ambivalent. Fatal in that she cannot reproduce, her insight occurs too late, thus the transgression into the uterine is *textual* and not historical/ social. Queen Christina is ultimately the Fe-Male Bisexual who transgresses into the female uterine, becoming a 'usurper of a feminine prerogative'.[32] Her discursively produced libidinal excess is an overflow of desires. Foucault's category of sex and identity are the effect and instrument of a regulatory sexual regime. But is that regulation reproductive or heterosexual? Does that regulation of sexuality produce male and female identities within a symmetrical binary relation? Does homosexuality produce sexual non-identity? Then homosexuality no longer relies on identities being *like* one another. But if homosexuality is meant to designate the place of an unnameable libidinal heterogeneity, is this a love that cannot or dare not speak its name? The fact is that 'sex does not cause gender, and gender cannot be understood to reflect or express sex'.[33] All gender is fictive and therefore citational. 'Garbo "got in drag" whenever she took some heavy glamour part, whenever she melted in or out of a man's arms, whenever she simply let that heavenly-flexed neck ... bear the weight of her thrown-back head ... How resplendent seems the art of acting! It is all *impersonation*, whether the sex underneath is true or not.'[34]

Queen Christina's desires are homo-social, homo-historical and overspill the binary-gendered space into two kinds of bi-sexualities, 'two opposite ways of imagining the possibility and practice of bisexuality'.[35] Bisexuality can be a fantasy of a complete being. Cixous relates this idea to 'Ovid's Hermaphrodite [...] not made up of two genders but of two halves. Hence a fantasy of unity. Two within one, and not even two wholes.'[36] Thus Christina's desire for a child is an acceptance of the differently gendered script that was imposed upon her life as she finally seeks to add a dimension to it that she is able to, with the body of a woman. In repudiating the destructive energy of the male, and replacing it with the creative energy of the female, Christina's resolution is one struggling toward an identity of metaphoric androgyny – in a blend of oppositions which is perhaps the most powerful and yet, most benign; that blend of duality which metaphysics describes as 'truth' and a one-ness of being; the Hegelian dialectic which, in a metaphysics of being, blends Apollo and Dionysius.

An alternative reading has us consider another bisexuality which is an inscription of alterity within the self: it is 'the location within oneself of the presence of both sexes, evident and insistent in different ways according to the individual, the non-exclusion of difference or of a sex, and starting with this "permission" one gives oneself, the multiplication of the effects of desire's inscription on every part of the body and the other body.'[37] Thus we see her as a competitive intellectual reflective male, where Christina realizes that in bringing forth life, in creating an additional dimension to her self, she will be able to surpass the men she has always identified with. The act of creation will bring her a power which is denied the biological male, a power which surpasses the one she is used to wielding. On this reading Queen Christina is a misogynist male – this is 'an emancipation of the oppressor in the name of the oppressed', when 'the female body [...] is freed from the shackles of the paternal law [proving] to be yet another incarnation of that law, posing as subversive but operating in the service of that law's self-amplification and proliferation.'[38] Or is the resolution of Queen Christina's identity an unexpected permutation which results in difference? Does she indicate a cultural possibility in the kaleidoscope of citational choice? 'If subversion is possible, it will be a subversion from within the terms of the law, through the possibilities that emerge when the law turns against itself and spawns unexpected permutations of itself. The culturally constructed body will then be liberated, neither to its "natural" past, nor to its original pleasures, but to an open future of cultural possibilities.'[39] Butler's Foucauldian-Lacanian explanation posits 'the culturally contradictory enterprise of the mechanism of repression [as] prohibitive and generative at once'[40] thus enabling two readings of Christina's identity resolution. '[The] overthrow of "sex" results in the release of a primary sexual multiplicity'[41] giving Christina a new identity formulated in citational difference. For man 'what is repressed is leaning toward one's own sex.' Thus it is *woman* who is truly bisexual, 'man having been trained to aim for glorious phallic monosexuality'. Woman benefits from and opens up this bisexuality 'which does not annihilate differences but cheers them on, pursues them, adds more.'[42] Queen Christina passes finally, on this reading, into a Cixousian excess, a 'spacious singing Flesh: onto which is grafted no one knows which I – which masculine or feminine, more or less human, but above all living, because changing I.'[43]

The story of Queen Christina is mythologized to make it symbolic for the shifting and queer identity of today's western woman. *Queen Christina* continues to be a powerful performance piece about gender identity which makes women – and men – confront the constructionality of their selves as we enter a twenty-first century of increased gender complexity.

The Binary Machine and the Liberation of Woman: Arthur and Guinevere

Guinevere to Arthur: You are a barbarian (II, p.15)

Where is she?
Activity / Passivity
Sun / Moon
Culture / Nature
Day / Night
(Hélène Cixous and Catherine Clément, *The Newly Born Woman*, p.63)

Guinevere: I've used my own judgement.
Arthur: WHO SAID YOU COULD DO THAT! (II, p.5)

The various versions of the legend of Arthur and Guinevere are well known. In some versions the legend depicts their undying love for each other; in others Guinevere has a lover, Lancelot. Sometimes Guinevere loves Lancelot; in other tales it is Arthur.

Gems opens her play with a typical shock technique: she mythmakes to mythbreak. Arthur's near monologue to Guinevere's accompanying silence is the opening scene. It is a court of law where Guinevere is being judged for infidelity. Her husband in a conjuring up of notions of masculine power, legitimacy and privilege is her judge, her jury and her prosecutor.

As her husband and as the power of the State, Arthur represents the power of inheritance, the consequences of the traffic in women and the promise of social privilege. Boorish and ineloquent, King Arthur is portrayed as a beastly man who is the ultimate patriarch in the worst conceptual sense of the conventionally masculine.

Guinevere has a lover, unnamed here, but apparently one of many. The play is a struggle between the conventionally unfaithful husband and the wife who demands her sexual and intellectual freedom. Here, Woman (Guinevere) is organized under an oppositional metaphor, but unlike traditional western literature, philosophy, criticism, centuries of representation and reflection, Guinevere's representation in this play undercuts the stereotypically chained woman. The dual hierarchical oppositions of activity/ passivity, sun/ moon, day/ night come into play as Gems reworks the Arthur-Guinevere legend to make it a metaphor for the centuries-old representation of Woman. They function as a pair of oppositions: a *couple*. 'Victory', says Cixous, 'always comes down to the same thing: things get hierarchical. Organization by hierarchy makes all conceptual organization subject to man. Male privilege, shown in the opposition between *activity* and *passivity*, which he uses to sustain himself.[44]

Gems spins a modern, almost 60s tale of love between a radical feminist and the stereotypical figure of feminist mythology: the unbending, violent, sexually voracious patriarch. Guinevere seems the mythical feminine: she represents and even commands the moon and the tides and the weather. However, the space of passivity which Guinevere ought by patriarchal discursive norms to occupy is repeatedly undercut by the author as she crafts her character. By gesture and through verbal and non-verbal discourse Guinevere displays her repeated defiance of her stereotypical position in patriarchy. The absent woman of male philosophical discourse rears her head in Gems' play, making her presence felt through her circumscribed roles of mother, queen, and wife, carving at the end a quasi-autonomous place for herself in the symbolic order designed for the male with his attendant stereotypical masculinities which make patriarchy what it is. In Arthur's domain, Guinevere 'does not exist, she can not-be; but there has to be something of her. He keeps, then, of the woman he is no longer dependant, only this space, always virginal, as matter to be subjected to the desire he wishes to impart.' This 'subordination of the feminine to the masculine order [...] gives the appearance of being the condition for the machinery's functioning'.[45]

This is the space of the woman's non-existence and her burial. Guinevere however threatens 'the stability of the masculine structure that passes itself off as eternal-natural, by conjuring up from femininity the reflections and hypotheses that are necessarily ruinous for the stronghold still in possession of authority.'[46]

How does she – indeed, can she? – crumble the rock upon which patriarchy and the phallic order has constructed itself?

Arthur: Debauchery!

Eroticism!

Within this kingdom … within this city … within the palace of Camelot … within even … so it is alleged, in the indictment, within the sanctity of the royal bed itself.

[…]

If any of the charges here presented is proved beyond reasonable doubt the penalties are clearly laid down.

One: mutilation.

Two: breaking on the wheel.

Three: hanging.

Four: quartering, with the head to be displayed till crow-picked, then crushed under a stone, the fragments to be strewn outside the boundaries of the realm. (I, p.8)

Guinevere calls upon the very elements to bear witness to her in the court of law over which Arthur presides. In 'Sorceress and Hysteric' Cixous and Clément speak of woman's alliance with nature. Influenced by Marcel Mauss' *A General Theory of Magic*, they contend that at the critical periods of women's lives such as puberty, during menstruation, childbirth and menopause they are at their magical peak, possessing powers that men cannot have. Thus we see Guinevere here allied to the normative structure as wife/ mother (which she has defied) but allied also 'with those natural disturbances, their regular periods, which are the epitome of paradox, order and disorder. [T]he sorceress conceives Nature, and woman, the periodic being, takes part in something that is not contained within culture.'[47]

Guinevere knows the double standards of patriarchy well: 'I have been imprisoned … I have been deprived of liberty, *not because I have committed adultery, but because I am a woman.*' (I, p.29, emphasis mine). The Law of the Father that contains Guinevere denies her a voice, seeks to criminalize and ostracize her; by her defiant infidelity she seeks to becoming the sexual equal of her husband, the King who strays often and as a matter of rule; and, she hypothesizes, if he can get his pleasures elsewhere, so can she even if it means bearing children that are not his. In this she surpasses him as her trespasses taint his heirs; *and even in being like him, she is still herself as her identity is not tied to being like him.* She is the moon and the tides and the air, all natural elements obey her; she commands magic which has her occupy the space of the eternal feminine, here with a voice and a role which is defiant and has a distinctly feminine identity. This breaking of bounds is still from the space of eternal femininity and the story-that-ends-well is modern in her espousal of women's and political issues in the kingdom.

However, the space of the eternal feminine which Guinevere occupies is one of contradictions. Whilst occupying the site of feminine excess where she commands the elements, she is not in linguistic or non-verbal terms the conventional feminine: 'Oho, can't have that, can we? The goddess, farting? The Myth, picking her nose? The Ineffable Mother, pissing in the alley? No, no. Having been graced with the honour of chalicing YOU into life we must, naturally, be divine!' (II, p.11)

Guinevere is a radical feminist. She believes in women cloning children to divest themselves of their need for men:

> We don't need you, we don't need you, we don't need you! We can breed ourselves, women breeding women … not men … not men … men aren't needed. We can breed women on our own, but we can't breed men because men aren't needed. What do you think of that? (II, p.27)

In this play we are able to see the reason for the early western radical feminist valorization of a world without men. Seeing themselves as the victims of rigidly hierarchical and violent patriarchies, they may have a case to make for themselves. However, Gems reveals, in this drama, Arthur's masculinity as an ideological construct: it is a particular effect of him as a warrior, and therefore in a rigidly male space where masculine norms formulate him; and also the conventions of early patriarchy where men had frequent sexual access to women. The resolution of the fairytale-myth is modern as Guinevere has a place on the council and she is on the side of welfare for single mothers. The play ends as Arthur and Guinevere present themselves as equal, 'separate' and 'side by side'. She 'can share the responsibilities.' And Arthur gives her a place on the council with a warning: 'When you get out of the kitchen, don't complain of the heat, that's all.' (II, p.44). Guinevere is the Medusa who turns a man to stone. Yet she is also man's muse: 'We have been frozen in our place between two terrifying myths: between the Medusa and the abyss. […] All you have to do to see the Medusa is look her in the face: and she isn't deadly. She is beautiful and she laughs.'[48] Shut out of the patriarchal system which contains her, Guinevere is 'the repressed that ensures the system's functioning.'[49] Yet she also exceeds the masculine space occupied by Arthur: her femininity is an effect of magic and power, and she overspills the space Arthur occupies as a male. Arthur in realising he needs Guinevere, accepting her as his equal, makes a space for her, in the personal realm as well as the political making Guinevere the victor as she is not merely equal but more.

Jonathan Gems sees this play as a 'modern version of Shakespeare's *The Taming of the Shrew* [wherein] Male and Female lock horns and struggle throughout the play until a new, modern understanding is finally achieved.'[50] Pam Gems takes 'once-upon-a-time', the tale wherein woman is the eternal passive and subverts it to make Guinevere the woman who questions her role as wife and mother to be equal to and overspill the boundaries of the law of the phallic order. Here, queer enters the traditional discourse of the male to displace it in accommodating the feminine as an equal.

Theatre as Polemic: Pasionaria

How many liberation struggles, from Algeria to Kenya, from India to Ireland, from Vietnam to South Africa, were waged by women as brave and uncompromising as these? – Robert Young, Postcolonialism: An Historical Introduction, Blackwells, 2001. p. viii.

Humanity was smaller in yet a third respect: Europeans were, on the whole, distinctly shorter and lighter than they are today [...] The scrawny, stunted, undrilled soldiers of the French Revolution were capable of a physical endurance equalled today only by the undersized guerrillas in colonial mountains. – Eric Hobsbawm, The Age of Revolution 1789 – 1848, Weidenfeld & Nicholson, 1962.

The play opens with the announcement of the return to Spain of socialist revolutionary Dolores Ibárruri (La Pasionaria) from Russia, after the death of General Franco. The demise of the fascist Franco and his regime (he died in 1977) leaves vestiges strongly reminiscent of Orwell's *1984*, which Gems' eldest son, Jonathan, scripted for the BBC a year before *Pasionaria* was staged in Newcastle in 1985, the year of the Miners' Strike. Directed by Sue Dunderdale, the parallel between Gems' historical subject and the emerging social mobility of the British working classes in post-war Britain was emphasized in the video they received as a blessing from La Pasionaria herself: 'an elderly, extremely beautiful woman, with uniquely focused asperity of the woman politician – forever trying to juggle personal and professional life.'[51]

The opening dialogue between the sweeper father and the educated academic daughter in post-Franco Spain parallels the rising dominance in English academe of the educated working classes: the Jimmy Porters of the 1970s and 80s.

Dolores: (As the Man bends [to sweep the street] once more: Leave it. (She laughs). You're paid by the hour, not the job.
Father: Those books of yours are making you dishonest.

Dolores: You shouldn't be sweeping the streets, you're a faceworker. They should give you something decent —
Father: I'm lucky to get —
Dolores: Lucky? (She grabs the broom as he makes to pick it up again, he gives her a clout over the head, without rancour, it sends her reeling.)
Father: Watch your mouth, Dolores. And keep away from that library, you'll be losing your own place next. (*La Pasionaria*, I. i. p.2)

Ironically their exchange also reflects the deterioration of academic standards as seen at the turn of our century in England. Chaucer's Oxford scholar is a thing of the past as academics count learning and teaching by the hour:

A CLERK ther was of Oxenford also,
That unto logyk hadde longe ygo.
[...]
For hym was levere have at his beddes heed
Twenty bookes, clad in blak or red,
Of Aristotle and his philosophie
Than robes riche, or fithele, or gay sautrie.
But al be that he was a philosopher,
Yet hadde he but litel gold in cofre;
But al that he myghte of his freendes hente,
On bookes and on lernynge he it spente
[...]
And gladly wolde he lerne and gladly teche.
(Geoffrey Chaucer, *The Canterbury Tales*)[52]

The dramatic discourse in Act I, scene ii splices time to evidence the exploitation of the masses during Franco's regime and parallels 1980s British exclusion of class.[53] Again, as in the 1990s Britain that is coetaneous with my analysis of Churchill's *Mad Forest*, Franco's Spain lacks spirituality:

A young lad of fragile appearance enters, a small coffin under his arm.

Father: — where you off to?
Dolores: (sour) What you got there? (Together)
Bonifacio: Me sister.
Dolores: (protest) Oh, not the littlun with the fair hair?
          Ah, what a shame, what a shame.
          [...]

Dolores: Getting killed don't count. Leaving six kids don't count.
Bonifacio: Five.
Dolores: What?
Bonifacio: (Juggling the coffin) Five now. (I. ii)

'Sisters and brothers, little Maid,
How many may you be?'
'How many? Seven in all,' she said,
And wondering looked at me.

[…]

'How many are you then,' said I,
'If they two are in heaven?'
Quick was the little maid's reply,
'O Master! We are seven.'

'But they are dead; those two are dead!
Their spirits are in heaven!'
'Twas throwing words away; for still
The little Maid would have her will,
And said, 'Nay, we are seven!' (William Wordsworth, 'We Are Seven')

The class divisions are as exacerbated as always in Britain:

Senora Lopez: How many more times! I will not not not drink from a pitcher like
               a common peasant! (I, iv, p.11)

So is 'class' or the aesthetics of taste, which may or not be distinguished from class:

Senora Lopez: (Sipping delicately) Quite a good wine this time.
Senor Lopez: (Knocking it back) Should be at the price. (Nods to Dolores,
               gooses her as she refills his glass.) Never does to buy rubbish.
               (Drains it again.) (I, iv, p.11)

The condescension is obvious in Europe as it is in Britain and certainly practised to
the extreme in countries like India especially today:

Senora Lopez: (Pinging the bell furiously) I will not put up with it, bad enough
               living in a filthy miners' town, horrible black creatures with their

> horrible eyes looming at you … (She picks up the knife and fork, turns for the joint. Dolores bobs up, grabs the joint and is gone) … everywhere you look, nothing but black filth … (I, iv, p.12)

The play delineates not only the class divide between the miners and the pit owners but the difficulties of the first unions who couldn't negotiate but had to sell out, with the miners often arrested for insubordination to the bosses. The young Dolores, a miner's wife who is political, follows with a brave massed protest of her own with the women and is also arrested. In prison she is put in a single cell after she mobilizes the women prisoners to stop working (sewing) as they aren't paid for it. Act I ends on Dolores's release as the Spanish monarchy falls and all political prisoners are set free.

Act II opens to a united majority of working-class people cheering Dolores as she speaks for them all. Being a woman does not deter her. As she takes the stand to speak in the newly formed Republic of Spain, it is obvious that conditions for the working classes have changed, if only temporarily. As a candidate for the Popular Front, Dolores is hunted down by the soldiers, only escaping as the myth of Pasionaria (Dolores) has become one in which she is demonized, and described with fangs and sharpened fingernails. The party of the people, the Popular Front is victorious, and the first thing Pasionaria does as Member of Parliament of the Republican government is to release all political prisoners.

Quite soon, however, there are rumblings as the Right fights to gain back power:

> I had six hundred workers in my factory – […] six hundred! Before I gave it all over to my son and came into parliament for a tenth of the income I was making.
>
> Six hundred wage packets! (II, p.37)

Pasionaria questions the fact that people who are privileged are governing for those like themselves.

The play ends on polemic which sits well on stage in the years of the Miners' Strike in Britain:

> Who are the true enemies of this country? Of any country?
>
> I say they are those who erode the freedoms of the people. Those who contemptuously believe that the people […] the People … have no voice, no rights … no say in their own lives.

[...]
Let me ask you this question.
Who, as representatives paid by the people, are you governing for?
Who are you governing *for?*
WHO ARE YOU GOVERNING FOR? (*Pasionaria,* The end).

The abrasive polemic the play ends on – Pasionaria's passionate political speech – strikes a chord in the discord and governmental politics of the year the miners struck. The play makes no apology for its didacticism and furious lambasting of governmental policies. Gardner opines that the play is 'uncompromisingly political' in the parallels it draws 'between the [...] miners' dispute and the uprising of the Austurian mining community just before the Spanish Civil War.' Gems said the long political speech was 'a calculated risk' as [m]ost people are not political [...] Political plays are unfashionable. [...] We live in a decadent age and the writing is witty, elusive and cynical. I think that is defeatist.'[54] In this play Gems reveals the overt politicization which subtexts most of her work. *Pasionaria* is a play about a modern myth: Dolores Ibárruri who fought tirelessly for the rights of the People in Spain. The class politics the play delineates make this a piece of queer mythology.

Icons and Whores

[Q]ueerness requires an understanding of individual identity that remains alert and responsive to the endless variety of positions in which the very notion of identity might be articulated. – Joseph Bristow, *Effeminate England*

The implication for feminism today is that there is a multiplicity of voices within the category of gender, within the general category of women. Pam Gems writes several plays about a specific gender category, writing within which must surely be most difficult, prototypical as prostitution has always been of the very nadir of womanhood, pigeon-holed and derided by even the self-styled expert, Simone de Beauvoir (see below). Within this category, Gems attempts to explore that radical space of indeterminacy and potentiality, the multiple voices which belong to woman-as-hetaira (Piaf), courtesan (Camille), and prostitute (Stas, Lola), blurring each of these categories. Taking a stereotyped role and revealing variation within it, Gems demonstrates the limitless variety of women within the specificity of that pigeon-holed profession which even Beauvoir attaches labels to. Gems' courtesans serve as a trope for that larger category – woman – and the plurality within. Gems presents each as occupant of a range of categories so the courtesan overspills the prototypical space she occupies, making her more than just a stereotype. The various queer identities of woman-as-courtesan/hetaira/whore is explored in this section.

Courtesan / Hetaira / Whore: Camille, Piaf, Stas, Lola

We have hetairas for the pleasures of the spirit, *pallages* **(concubines) for sensual pleasure, and wives to give us sons**. – *Demosthenes, as quoted by Beauvoir.*[55]

The Second Sex is hailed by western feminists as one of the first feminist classics and has been translated widely. Published in 1949 and translated into English in 1953, the book has a pre-eminent place in feminist philosophy and gender theory.[56] However, Beauvoir problematizes the category of 'woman' by perpetuating the fact that women, by the rules of patriarchy, are already labelled or stereotyped as inhabiting one or the other of the tidy categories she sets out to describe. Her categories echo patriarchy: 'The Married Woman'; 'The Mother'; 'Prostitutes and Hetairas'. Although Beauvoir's method is historiographic, she seems to add to myths rather than dispel them: in the section labelled 'Prostitutes and Hetairas', having defined hetaira as 'high class' in relation to the 'common prostitute', she goes on to state definitively:

> I use the word hetaira to designate all women who treat not only their bodies but their entire personalities as capital to be exploited. Their attitude is very different from that of creative workers who, transcending themselves in the work they produce, go beyond the given and make their appeal to a freedom in others for which they open the doors to the future. The hetaira does not reveal the world, she opens no avenues to human transcendence; on the contrary, she tries to captivate the world for her own profit. (TSS 580)

Placing creative workers and hetairas in two binary categories, she proceeds to place models, actresses, movie stars, as well as dancers as twentieth-century occupants of the space vacated by the nineteenth-century 'distinguished' high-class courtesan. Whilst recognising that an amount of 'ability' is required, she continues:

> But for the vast majority of women an art, a profession, is only a means: in practising it they are not engaged in genuine projects. (TSS 585)

Representation can be endless as one attempts to portray the plurality of one half of the population. The task becomes more difficult when the attempt is to re-present those regarded as un-representable: the bawd, the harlot, the whore and the vamp are only ever presented in terms of the prototypal stereotype of the fallen woman, and Beauvoir falls into the same patriarchal fallacy of describing these women as useless. This is not 'woman as the area of limitless possibility' or 'a permanently contested site of meaning' unless one is punning on their profession. Diane Elam asserts in *Feminism and Deconstruction: Ms. en Abyme*, 'her-story is not one story. An injustice is committed when any *one* history purports to speak for all women everywhere',[57] when any one label excludes women from belonging to another category as histories overlap, 'there are always several histories in several places at once, there are always several histories underway; this is a high point in the history of women.'[58]

It was Aphra Behn – the first Englishwoman to 'earn her bread' by her writing – who initially re-presented a non-stereotyped woman-as-courtesan. During the latter half of the seventeenth century, a time when drama was as bawdy and licentious as it was in the closing years of the twentieth, the stage was still the patriarchal fold of male writers. Being a woman bold enough to write under her own name, Behn also prefaced her plays with cries against the gender-based injustice she faced. In one of her blunt epistles to the reader she declaimed:

> The play had no other misfortune but that of coming out for a Womans: had it been owned by a Man, though the most Dull Unthinking Rascally Scribler in Town, it had been a most admirable play. (Epistle to *Sir Patient Fancy*, 1678)

Behn's plays attacked several prevalent evils of her time, forced marriage being one such convention vituperatively opposed in *The Town Fop; or, Sir Timothy Tawdrey* (1676) and in *The Lucky Chance; or, An Alderman's Bargain* (1686). Behn uses the character of the prostitute 'as a weapon in her thematic attack on mercenary marriage',[59] and she figures this stock character in several plays as a foil to the good woman or the 'virgin' prototype (as is Angellica in *The Rover*, 1677). The 'Rover series' of plays illustrates the idea that prostitution may well be a more honest way to economic independence than mercenary arranged marriages. However, most of Behn's courtesans have a wish to marry, like the virtuous good woman of the play, although on a more non-stereotypical note the woman who 'wins' the man is the wittier and more generous hearted of the two, regardless of the stereotyped niche she occupies.

Gems, younger by almost exactly three centuries and as successful on the British stage, is as subversive and entertaining as was Behn. Gems' harlots range from the coarse street language of Piaf amidst the glamour of her successful career as a singer, contrasting with the glamour of Camille made complex by Camille's attachment to her son revealing motherhood and whoredom as synonomous, co-existent within one woman; the three different faces of prostitution in *The Treat* and the contemporary Stas – intellectual, amoral, independent. Gems delineates the queer category of woman-as-whore in these plays.

The Tragedy of Camille

La Dame aux Caméllias, a novel by Alexandre Dumas, *fils* (1852); Verdi's *La Traviata* (1853); actresses Sarah Bernhardt, Stella Patrick Campbell, and the Violetta of Verdi's opera on the stages of Paris and London, and Garbo, once again, to haunt on film. The passion, the life and the amours of the Lady of the Camellias have a long tradition in the limelight, glamorizing the lifestyle of a courtesan, 'recruiting' as George Bernard Shaw would put it, 'for Mrs. Warren's Profession'. K. Worth accuses Gems for writing a play along the lines of the popular novel, opera and Hollywood tradition of the glamorous and tear-jerking Camille: 'Gems is in tune with her romantically minded predecessors rather than with Shaw ['s indictment of poverty which forces the underpaid, undervalued, overworked woman to turn to prostitution]'.[60] Shaw's trenchant pen wrote: 'Plays about prostitution [showed the courtesan as] beautiful, exquisitely dressed and sumptuously lodged', rather than the poor, destitute women they really were.[61] Indeed Shaw satirised the upper classes for their hypocrisies toward prostitutes and also toward the patronage of plays which portrayed the courtesan's life as one to be desired in his 1854 play, *Mrs. Warren's Profession*, which the Lord Chamberlain immediately censored. But Gems' play is, like all her work, utterly subversive as it undercuts the dominant ideology from within the play.

> Viewed from the standpoint of economics, [the] position [of the prostitute] corresponds with that of the married woman. In *La Puberté* Marro says: 'The only difference between women who sell themselves in prostitution and those who sell themselves in marriage is in the price and the length of time the contract runs'.

Beauvoir, in obvious agreement with Marro, continues:

> For both the sexual act is a service; the one is hired for life by one man; the other has several clients who pay her by the piece. The one is protected by one male against all others; the other is defended by all against the exclusive tyranny of each. (TSS 569)

Yet, the path of the prostitute, compared to that of the married woman seems one of relative independence, and this is borne out by the women of the play who live in a supportive woman-centred world. Toward the close of the play, Prudence informs the grieving Armand: 'Has it never occurred to you that some of us might prefer the life – given the alternatives?' (*Camille,* II, vii) The alternatives are poverty, or the life of a married woman which to the relatively 'free' courtesan spelt slavery. However, 'neither wife nor hetaira succeeds in exploiting a man unless she achieves an individual ascendancy over him.' (TSS 569) *Camille* is the story of one woman's singular power – 'individual ascendancy' – over a man. It is a story which has all the elements of a passion play and sentimental melodrama which Gems carefully avoids by the skilfully worked out structure of the play. Transposing scenes rapidly in her hallmark filmic cuts, Gems presents the play so the future precedes the past, thus presenting scenes which would make for histrionics before the causal events have occurred. The dramatization succeeds in avoiding the overwhelming melodrama of the novel and the opera by a feat of dramatic technique which closely resembles the short scenes and jump-starts of film. The opening scene, set in her bedchamber in a conflation of personal and public, is an auction of Marguerite Gautier's personal effects after her death. Her lover, Armand, wanders onto a scene of what amounts to a symbolic and public rape as the auctioneer pauses significantly over her bed:

> And now ... the lot you've all been waiting for ... the bed. Decorated with – ah ... (he consults his list) ... camellias. What was it ... twenty three days of the month she wore white camellias and for the other five days she wore red ... (I, i)

The opening is thus a demythologizing as it demystifies the glamour by focusing on what is still a taboo of the female body: menstruation. As the bed is bid for, Armand collapses in anguish. A lover's (private) discourse mingles cruelly with that of the (public) material world of economics in the strata of the demi-monde. As Llewellyn-Jones puts it, the 'condensation of sexuality and economics' is 'indicated semiologically in the opening scene': a gest which 'underlies all the emotional transactions' of the play.[62]

The next scene moves back in time, cutting to the moment of their first meeting. Armand is revealed as a stereotypical male, in the pursuit of women, and also cruel and given to the abuse of the courtesans whose company he seeks. This is a regular client, not material for a romance. Sophie, who appears to be an enchantment he has tired of, has returned from what could only have been a dangerous abortion. Bela, Armand's companion, mocks her cruelly:

> Bela: Where have you been?
> Sophie: If you must know, I've been to Dieppe.
> Bela: Dieppe? ... The end of the universe! A long way to buy a crochet hook
>   ... (I, ii)

Armand seems to have had liaisons with most of the other courtesans as well, and, having tired of them all is ready for a new distraction who does not 'disappoint'. This is the moment when Marguerite appears to make a lasting impression on the rover:

> There is a long still pause as they regard each other. She inclines her head the merest fraction and walks away. He gazes after her then turns to PRUDENCE. As he does so, MARGUERITE turns to see him go. (Stage directions)

Marguerite Gautier is to all appearances the hetaira as described by Beauvoir:

> There are many degrees between the common prostitute and the high class hetaira. The essential difference is that [the hetaira] endeavours to gain recognition for herself – as an individual – and if she succeeds, she can entertain high aspirations. Beauty and charm or sex appeal are necessary here, but are not enough: the woman has to be distinguished … She will have 'arrived' … only when the man has brought her worth to the attention of the world. In the last century it was her town house, her carriage, her pearls … (TSS 578)

As Roland Barthes later put it, obviously reading Beauvoir's existentialist text alongside the myth of Camille, 'the central myth […] is not Love, it is Recognition.'[63] The existentialist position of Marguerite's class (Slave) to Armand's (Master) elicits Barthes' comparison with women from lower classes accrued onto Beauvoir's earlier parallel with the married woman: 'the alienation of Marguerite Gautier in relation to the class of her masters is not fundamentally different from that of today's petit-bourgeois women in a world which is just as stratified.' The hierarchization of society necessitates Marguerite to need Recognition from the world of her masters, Armand's class and also the middle-class audiences where 'the grateful and recognizing gaze of the bourgeois class is […] delegated to the [audience] who in [their] turn *recognize* Marguerite.' Barthes sees the mythology of this love as two separate ideologies: it is two separate types of love which stem from two different positions in society. The master's love is 'eternal' as it is valorized by the world of the masters themselves, whilst the slave is alienated *and also aware of her alienation.* The ideology of her love is constructed as a response to the world of the masters: 'either she plays the part which the masters expect from her, or she tries to reach a *value* which is in fact a part of this same world of the masters.' This value is attained by Marguerite in the sacrifice of her love, which was also, like the love, endorsed by the same world. Thus Marguerite undergoes, in the awareness of her complete estrangement, a kind of erasure of self, as she exists only as a response to the ideals of a world she can never belong to.[64]

In reaching the 'value' of the world of the masters Marguerite 'proves' her love is ideal: i.e., non-material. Even when Armand is cut off from his inheritance she stays by him.

She may be the distinguished hetaira of Beauvoir's classification, but her origins are common. Born in poverty, sexually abused before the age of five, seduced and impregnated by her master, the Marquis (who is also Armand's father), she took her opportunity where she found it as she escaped to Paris with luxuries stolen from her master's house.

> 'When a door has once been broken open, it is hard to keep it shut', said a young prostitute of fourteen, quoted by Marro. [...] Now that she no longer belongs to one man, she feels she can give herself to all. (TSS 571–572)

Hard to keep the door shut, also, when the men in the courtesan's milieu display by word and action their lack of respect: in scene i it is the auctioneer, in scene ii, Armand and Bela, and in scene iii the valet who spits in disgust at the sight of Janine and Marguerite locked in a catfight. Since the beginning of 'civilization' there have existed prostitutes in patriarchal societies to satisfy the prototypical man's desires. Compartmentalizing lust and love, patriarchy divided its women into virgins and whores, as the latter, though used to satiate lust, is also the repository of every negative value, and is often abused. In the repeated verbal and visual signs of abuse in the play, Gems demonstrates that – like Shaw – she is concerned at revealing the hypocrisy of society. She deconstructs the dominant ideology from within the guise of a West End show, wherein lies the genius of her subversion. The hypocrisy is revealed at its height in the words of the Marquis (the same man who had abused Marguerite and fathered her child) to his son, Armand:

> Respect? Respect?! For a whore!! You dare to talk of love … you dare to talk of friendship – with a whore? [...] Introduce a harlot? Into my family? Are you seriously suggesting … that you want … as your life's companion … before God and the Church … as the mother of your children … as my heirs … a woman who has felt the private parts of every man in Paris? (II, i)

Having thus posited her female protagonist within the specificity of a typecast profession in a cruel, hegemonic, masculist culture who does not hesitate to revile her almost on cue, Gems draws the ropes of middle-class values tightly, and Marguerite Gautier with them.

Armand, in love with one patriarchal category as it were – the whore – now attempts to re-posit his love back into a prelapsarian mode. He is struck with Marguerite immediately – the myth of love at first sight – and rebukes her for the vulgar nature of the song sung by her. Her answer is in complete awareness of her alienated existentialist position; coldly, honestly she replies with irony: 'What would you have me sing? Something more elevated? Don't delude yourself, Monsieur'. (I, iii)

> Most prostitutes are morally adapted to their mode of life. Not that they are immoral congenitally or by heredity, but they feel integrated … in a society that manifests a demand for their services. They know very well that the edifying lecture of the police sergeant who registers them is pure verbiage, and elevated sentiments proclaimed by their clients … do little to intimidate them. (TSS 577)

Marguerite, typically unintimidated, distinguishes herself from the other courtesans who are too cloying for Armand. This aloofness combined with her stunning beauty make her infinitely desirable in Armand's eyes and his fascination wraps the narrative in the web of myth. Through the play, as in the last cited scene, Gems de-mythicizes 'romance, revealing it as a construct masking the exploitative nature of the traditional notions of sexuality.'[65]

The mythology of love encoded in the play is ensured by a series of devices: firstly, Marguerite's early demise whilst Armand is still in the passionate throes of love guarantees that she is instantly and forever unattainable: an impossible ideal enshrined in his passion. While she lived she swung between rational materiality and impulsive love: unwilling to abandon a carefully constructed life of comfort, economic security, and above all, independence from the tyranny of being dependant for all her wants on a single man; yet, carried away with Armand's vision of a future together. Always aware that men like Armand tired of the objects of their distraction quickly (as he indeed proved, in the first scene of their meeting) Marguerite treads warily: 'Cinderella does not always dream of Prince Charming; whether husband or lover, she is afraid he might turn into a tyrant …' (TSS 580). Also aware of the vast gulf of class between them, she voices her awareness of her alienation:

> … no! There is no world, no way that you and I can connect … except in the moment … There is nothing for us. I could look over the wall at you all my life and never get to touch your coat-tails. Don't be a fool. Only a fool believes a lie. (I, vi)

'It is a very particular state of myth, defined by [...] a parasitic awareness'. This awareness makes her more rather than less resistant to his charm, making her unattainable in life, elevating her far above the other demi-mondaines in his eyes.

The cause of her early death is consumption: she is that 'one in twenty [who] has tuberculosis ... [one of the] forty per cent [who] die before the age of forty' (TSS 585). Then as now, prostitutes were the most vulnerable to the plethora of fatal infections caught from their clients, and the beautiful Marguerite is no exception. The final brush strokes in the construction of this myth which has played for a century on European stages, is the fact that Marguerite is first a mother. Jean-Paul is her only constant in her world of ever changing affections and it is this love that the Marquis is able to buy so she can accomplish what Barthes calls 'the murder of the courtesan she is' and along with that the 'indirect murder of Armand's passion'.[67] Llewellyn-Jones accuses Gems for mythologizing 'the essentialist notion that motherhood is true fulfilment and its loss [...] inevitably tragic.'[68] Although it is true that a number of Gems' plays reflect on motherhood, it is part of women's condition, and, here, it is part of the original mythical narrative as it provides the fatal twist in the 'plot' snatching Marguerite away from Armand, as she attempts to buy her son 'the myth of respectability'.[69]

'The mismatch between the mythic construct of romance and the materialism of reality is encoded through various devices in the [...] text'.[70] Marguerite has been big business: as the appropriately named Mme. Prudence reflects, 'You keep us all afloat ... servants, seamstresses, shoemakers ... not a bad achievement for a girl who couldn't write her own name.' (II, iii). This is the life Marguerite returns to, as Act II, scene ii reveals the fickleness of her world. Janine is Madame's new protégée: as one star fades, a new beauty quickly replaces it; in a world where variety is of essence, the old star is quickly forgotten.

Gems maintains a delicate balance in her portrayal of Armand. His undying passion for the beautiful courtesan coupled with his illusionistic notions of an ideal life with her make this cruel, violent man maddeningly human. By presenting him at the opening scene at his most vulnerable, Gems unties him from occupying a stereotyped, gendered, masculinist role. His violence towards Marguerite when he discovers she is considering one more night with the Russian prince for his emeralds, to enable the lovers to buy their freedom, leaves Marguerite hysterical and distraught, but the scene is poignant as the audience is aware that he will never see her alive again. This is his last meeting with his ideal love before her quiet death. Again, his sentimental desire to have her remains moved to the family vault against the advice of his closest friends, as also his marked and genuine anguish at the loss of his love, balance the hateful side to his nature.

James Redmond calls Camille 'a 'useful play' which reclaim[s] the truth about women's lives from 'the dustbins of male historians' [as Gems] offers a feminist account of the sex-war [of] violent intensity'.[71] The final de-construction of the myth in the text's multiple interrogative strategies, reveals, however, that 'death is the penalty for those women who defy the norms of status, materialism and sex'[72] as Gems reassesses 'the reality behind the fairytales.'[73] The queer categories of class and woman-as-hetaira are explored in this play as in *Piaf.*

The Legend of Edith Piaf

Like the courtesan Marguerite Gautier, the Sparrow Piaf's origins are 'common', but she holds on to all signs of being working class with a tenacious ferocity throughout her meteoric rise to success as the highest paid woman singer in the world. The play is, as Wandor notes, about a basic 'gutter survival' and 'faith in women's basic resilience.'[74] Pam Gems said, 'I didn't think they'd really do it since it's a bit rude.' The reviewer Peters notes, 'it's not "a bit rude" – it's *filthy* [...] Pam Gems has the rare talent to push the boundaries of acceptability.'[75]

Piaf's is a portrait of 'a woman for whom female independence means an active and vigorous sexuality, which at its most intense parallels the orgasmic satisfaction she gets from singing, and a bristly, individualistic identification with being working class.'[76] The demythologizing of the star begins, in characteristic Gems fashion, with the first scene, where, as in the later *Camille*, the playwright uses the cinematic-dramatic technique of transposition of the past into the present to capture Piaf at the downslide of her career. Her talent numbed in the web of heroin addiction, Piaf is caught in the spotlight – centre stage – unable to perform. Through the play she is constantly distanced as Other in the use of her coarse language, and her first words are the characteristic defensive: 'Get your fucking hands off me, I ain't done nothing yet ...'

Piaf is an unsettling mix of heady glamour and backstreet crudity, enormous talent couched in verbal and non-verbal coarseness and vulgarity. Her talent enables her to be picked off the street to be given the opportunity to sing in a classy Parisian nightclub. Like Marguerite and the 1996 dramatization of Marlene Dietrich, this character escapes Beauvoir (and patriarchy)'s tidy categorization of glamorous stars – the modern-day hetairas – who feed off men to ensure their success (TSS 578–9). Through the play we see Piaf surrounded by people who make their living from her talent: from her managers to the young men who want to sing with Piaf, live with Piaf, look at Piaf, they are all drawn by the lure of ringing cash registers – theirs. But the hard-headed, tough-minded streetwise Piaf takes a 'genuinely greedy pleasure … when she [can] afford to pay for any man she desire[s], instead of having to oblige any man who desire[s] her.'[77]

In scene ii Gems transposes time to give us the young Edith walking the streets of Paris before the advent of her singing career. She has the same coarseness she will display at the height of her fame, and she responds to Leplée with her standard, '*Get your fucking hands off me, I ain't done nothing* …' Independent, defiant and self-willed, a woman who stands her own ground no matter what the situation, used to the hard life of working the streets, she assumes the nightclub manager expects sexual favours for the money he gives her. It does not occur to her or to her friend, Toine, that she has a talent for something other than selling her body for sex.

The friendship between Piaf and Toine establishes a female solidarity, and gives her personal life a continuity in the play which spans her life. They share an intimate easy rapport born of a sisterhood formed whilst working clients together.

> … prostitutes have a close solidarity among themselves; they may happen to be rivals, to feel jealous, to hurl insults at one another, to fight; but they profoundly need one another to form a counter-universe in which they regain their human dignity. The comrade is the preferred confidante and witness; it is she who will appreciate the dress and the coiffure intended for man's seduction but which seem like ends in themselves under the envious or admiring gaze of other women. (TSS 575)

Toine seems to be the Simone Berteaut of Piaf's acquaintance; 'Momone' who later claimed to be her sister. They were street singers together: in a culture where the profession has been highly honourable[78] much as India's temple prostitutes were considered sacred. There are long gaps – sometimes years – which separate their meetings, but what binds them is their past and their class origins. Piaf, despite herself, has acquired the trappings of glamour and success, and towards the end appears different from Toine who has ended up more conventionally – married with three children. The war years allow them to rearticulate the old camaraderie as they are happy to do their bit for the war effort, i.e., letting the soldiers have it gratis. Her friend Marlene Dietrich, who appears in the later *Marlene* has the same nonchalant attitude as she, too, provides 'comfort for the troops' (*Marlene*, I, p.20) Although in the end the two old acquaintances (Toine and Piaf) seem to have nothing in common anymore, the intervening years having brought Piaf success beyond their youthful dreams, they still share a strong bond of identification. Realising that

> ... they all want a slice, even the bloody managers. Will they take the rough with the smooth, will they hell! (II, vi)

She, like Marlene, has her bond of female solidarity which goes back into the past. She shares her passion for her craft with Marlene, who, after the war, made a few more movies and then became a cabaret and concert performer.[79]

> They want the bloody product, they want that all right, all wrapped up with a feather in its ass, but songs – what do they know about songs! (*Piaf*, II, vi)

> Yah ... agents, managers ... fog, strike, crisis – "Take the Concorde, be here yesterday" ... in the end, your work, the thing you dedicated your life to, denied yourself, lost friends for ... the work – that becomes remote ... immaterial. (*Marlene*, I, p.23)

Strong, self-willed, independent, these stars are not Garbo: 'Grrreta Garrrbo. Always on the screen like she is suffering some female problem down below' (ibid.); nor are they Beauvoir's courtesans: 'A lifetime of marriages? Not for me. I'd rather sell pumpernickel.' (ibid., p.24) These are icons who know where it's at: ' ... Nah, pretty soon they're not going to want my stuff. My sort's dying out. Going extinct. What they want now is discs. Canned. In the can ...' (*Piaf*, II, vi) Piaf knows she isn't going to be on top forever. As at the beginning, Piaf seems to be in it for one thing – the men she will have as a result of the fame, the success, the money. Her first thought when she is paid as a star is for 'the little guy down the garage. I could get him a ... suit ... coat, cufflinks, silk shirts' (I, v). She cheerfully shares her earnings with Toine giving her a generous half share. Piaf never succeeds in polishing her speech patterns or, indeed, in cleaning up her vocabulary. She dates relatively upper-class men at first, like Paul in Act I, scene v who attempt to 'cultivate' her:

> Paul: You don't have to stay in the gutter just because you were born there.
> Piaf: I feel out of place! I'm doing like what you said ... trying to be a lady ...
>   [*she becomes aware of her own voice, and shrivels in her seat*]. (I, v. Emphasis mine)

It is this class divide, one that Piaf is desperate to bridge at first, and later resents, which elicits from her the rage and derision she feels for the bourgeoisie. Her attitude to her secretary – 'that middle-class bitch' (II, iii) – is purposely mocking and scornful, as Piaf seethes with resentment.

The private self of Piaf is Piaf on stage, in a strangely class-based dis-play of a private discourse of the body and sexuality. Early on in her career, she is warned by her more sophisticated beaux: 'Piaf, your private life is your private life. Don't mix it.' (I, v). However, the public is, for Piaf, an expression of the personal, as throughout the play both are inseparably imbricated in each other. The morphology traverses the public spaces of the backstreet, the entertainment stages, the war spaces, each of which is indelibly stamped on by Piaf's private excesses. The most memorable scene, one which transforms this play into contemporary myth, is the one when the young Piaf, faced with an unfamiliar 'posh' setting, sips from the finger bowl arousing the waiter's scorn. Rebuffed for her *faux pas*, she defiantly lifts her skirts as she urinates in public atop the table in the restaurant: 'All right clever cock. Seen me drink – now you can watch me piss.'[80] Unable to detach herself from her art, for Piaf every performance is an orgasm, as she comes with and for the audience:

Piaf:	When I go on to do a song, it's me that comes on. They get the lot … they see what they're getting – everything I got.
Josephine:	Sure. But learn how to save it.
Piaf:	Nah.
Josephine:	Kid, you can't have an orgasm every single time you walk on stage.
Piaf:	I can.
Josephine:	No you can't. Nobody can. Nobody peaks all the time. Technique, baby! Trust it. Let it work for you. That way you don't exhaust yourself all the time … (II, i)

Yet this is the very quality which made Piaf so popular and so wanted – her complete and utter absorption in her work – an absorption which is a 'play' and a joy: a *jouissance* of the spirit-as- body as she offers 'the grain of the voice'.

The scenes in act II are short cinematic-style cuts of Piaf's colourful life: Piaf at the height of her fame, Piaf ravaged by heroin, Piaf's young boys whose performances she tries to transfer, usually unsuccessfully, to the stage; her lover, the boxer Marcel Cerdan's death in a plane crash; the driving accidents and heroin addiction she surfaces from, time and again, to return to the stage to sing and fascinate her audiences once more. The eighth scene of the second act is a reprise of the opening scene: her dependence on drugs has finally destroyed her ability to perform. As she ruins performance after attempted performance she has to be dragged off the stage unceremoniously – '*get your fucking hands off me* …' The last two scenes show Piaf with friends – she has, over the period of her life, built lasting friendships, and is fortunate to have had young men like Jacko sincerely care; and this scene has a caring Jacko ready to cancel his tour to be by her side during her hospitalization. It is here, too, that she meets the young Greek, Theo, whom she later marries and also performs with in yet another comeback. That is Piaf's career: a series of ever successful comebacks, a modern legend whose songs stir and delight. Gems' last scene shows us a Piaf who has all she longed for and more: a young man to love, her friendship with Toine as well as a lasting fame. In a profession which leaves lesser equipped mortals lonely, cynical and bitter, Piaf's is a significant victory. The play closes on Piaf as a twentieth-century western myth as she sings '*Je ne regrette rien*' with characteristic raw emotion.

If it is Edith Piaf one wants, then perhaps more than any other play (including *Marlene*), *Piaf* is better seen in performance than de-constructed as performative possibility off the page. The quality of the songs and the absorption and emotional intensity of Piaf's stage presence make for memorable characterization read best when encoded in a discourse of 'a body that matters'. Thus the success of Elaine Paige 'materialized' as Piaf:

> Paige … sings … not in direct imitation of Piaf but with something of her fierce attention to their emotional content.[81]

> When she sings Piaf [Elaine Paige] soars … those of us lucky enough to have seen her in person at Olympia in Paris have always felt the same: no regrets.[82]

However, the play itself – a subversive and creative re-presentation of a successful life and a de-construction of what goes into the making of a modern legend – was dismissed collectively by a number of broadsheet reviewers as 'sketchy … scrappy';[83] dire with 'tripey dialogue';[84] 'fragmented';[85] a 'sketchy trawl through [thirty] years of her subject's bumpy life'.[86] Elaine Paige, more of a singer/ performer than an actor had overwhelmed the audiences with her singing which may have rather overshadowed the script.

> Why not just an evening of Paige sings Piaf? It would be ten times more enjoyable and save a fortune in scenery.[87]

> … one of the great star-turns of the year, if not the decade. Hall and Paige … [have turned the play] into a breathtaking musical triumph by the simple device of focusing on the songs rather than the dialogue.[88]

This is where the critical strategy of reading performativity off the page demonstrates its worth. A new play by a new dramatist – two new stars on the horizon of English drama. However, a performance reading of the Elaine Paige production, as demonstrated to a certain extent by the broadsheet reviewers, fails to even acknowledge an excellent dramatic text by a dramatist who demonstrates the flair for popular acclaim with subversive political intent. For an intensive reading of the deep structure of a dramatic text, performativity must necessarily be read off the page from the multiple points of view of a director, actor and critic. Thus in terms of reconstructing the 'better' production, it is necessary also to point the way to more possibilities.

The original 1978 production of the play had Jane Lapotaire play Piaf.[89] She not only 'took *Piaf* from Stratford to the West End [but] to Broadway, where she won a Tony award'.[90] Lapotaire was not a singer and the difference between the two productions was that 'at the RSC fifteen years ago, [*Piaf*] came over as a sketchy, but authentic portrait of a gutter genius, whose gift had to be taken on trust.'[91] Thus, for the play to 'work' the singing has to take a back seat, and is therefore ideally 'against the grain'. Or, as the later strategy used for *Marlene*, all the songs – what the West End audiences actually pay for – could come right at the end. *Marlene*, another Gems act of subversive triumph, had Sian Phillips sing – beautifully – lots of 'Dietrich' after the play. This strategy worked well – the body of the voice, coming as it did after the entertaining but political statement of gender, sexuality, friendship and myth, had the audiences delay their primary gratificatory source.

Piaf was the first play written by a (contemporary) woman to be produced by the RSC. It is a play drawn in a series of rapid sketches which reveal Piaf's rapid rise to fame and her subsequent deterioration symbolically and efficiently. The mythical status of this star was ironically echoed in one reviewer's comment on the closing song: 'numbingly predictable'.[92] Gems, in fact, chose the songs with care, and most were the lesser known of Piaf's repertoire. This made the play a success in Britain, while the same contributed to bad press in the United States.[93]

Jonathan Gems adds: '*Piaf* is Pam Gems' most commercially successful play so far. Since its first production by the Royal Shakespeare Company in 1977, it has had 23 productions in the UK alone. It has been produced in many countries, including China and Japan, and has always been successful with audiences […] often winning "best actress" awards for the actress playing Edith Piaf. Interestingly, the only city where the play has not been a hit was Paris, Piaf's home-town.' *Piaf* was the play which enabled the RSC to break the bounds from subsidised theatre to the commercial West End. The first play to transfer from the small studio stage of the Other Place to the large RSC Aldwych, *Piaf* received offers from commercial West End producers. In a radical departure, the RSC under the direction of Trevor Nunn produced the play at the Piccadilly Theatre in London and, later, negotiated its transfer to the Plymouth Theatre on Broadway leading to further partnerships between the RSC and West End and Broadway managements. 'One abiding memory Pam Gems has of *Piaf* was of a production in Philadelphia which she visited. Standing at the back of the theatre with the Front of House Manager during a performance, she noticed that the half-dozen usherettes who had been selling programmes and showing people to their seats before the start of the show, were all up in the "gods" watching the play. When Gems remarked on this, the Front of House Manager said they did this every night, which was unusual because they had never done it before. Usually, when the show was running, they were in the café.'[94]

The popularity of Gems' Piaf stems from her ability to write a character who defies categorization, emerging as a subject constituted in apparently conflictual discourses – not a 'whore' (cf. Beauvoir) nor a typical 'star'. She is a hard-headed, foul-mouthed survivor who is prone to emotional vulnerability; generous hearted, insensitive, intense, she has the ability to enjoy life to the fullest with no regrets, and a knack for bouncing back from each catastrophe with a vigour and a verve which characterizes her dichotomousness. This is another Gems statement on womanhood which defies labels and goes against the normative grain. By positing the Piaf who walked the streets of mid-thirties Belleville on the high of success without polishing her rough edges or vulgar tongue, Gems manages to portray her as yet another woman who occupies that multifarious region peopled with characters with as much variety as human beings are capable of re-citing.

Woman as Controlling Subject: The Blue Angel

The club performer in Piaf is paralleled by *The Blue Angel*'s Lola – equally rough and common, Lola is a singer who ensnares the heart of Professor Unraat, and the Professor's love for her leads to his destruction.

Based on the 1905 novel *Professor Unraat* by Heinrich Mann and influenced by the 1930s film *The Blue Angel* starring Marlene Dietrich as Lola, Gems spins a skilful drama which typically does not unveil the desirous Lola in the first scene.[95] The audience of The Blue Angel club is raucous with cries demanding her presence but she doesn't make an appearance just yet. This mystery is sustained as we move to the professor's teaching class as his character is neatly unfolded for the audience. He is harsh, disciplining the boys, but, in turn, cowed by the headmaster. This is a hierarchy maintained in the play when the professor loses his social status as his peers keep their prestige. Lola also makes her presence felt in the second scene in the classroom in a verse written by one of the boys. Scene iii has the professor stalking his charges in an attempt to catch them red-handed with what he suspects is a disreputable entertainment troupe, and he finds himself in The Blue Angel club. Here the mystery of the enchanting Lola is maintained as 'she appears with her back to' the audience, and the spirit of Marlene Dietrich is evoked in the writing. It is perhaps in this play most of all that we see Gems fascination with film in her youth.

> I suppose mine was the first generation – in the twenties – to grow up with the movies as an integral part of life. We didn't stop reading [but this was] supported by three times a week to the local Regent Cinema. [...] We were the stars. Blundering out into the high street from *Malibu*, *Old Vienna* or *42nd Street*, you found yourself walking high shouldered like Joan, or tossing curls like Ginger. How can we say that we aren't embued, infected by it all?[96]

she wrote years later in her introduction to the play about Marlene Dietrich. The mystery of Marlene of the film overshadows the writing of this piece as Lola enters. Her provocative appearance is as in the schoolboy Eberhardt's verse: Lola is 'lithe, ordinary, leveleyed and laughing' and her audience adores her as does her manager Bombler and several others who are fascinated by her charm. She may be ordinary but her audience is too. She may have been played by Dietrich in the film but there is a sleazy air to the club and to Lola. Her admirers are schoolboys and the bumbling manager and an audience comprised of navvies who haven't seen a woman for a while. This is no film star but an ordinary woman who spells sex and seduction in a small town devoid of any. She is adept at playing on the schoolboys' adoration: kissing one's palm she folds it over, whispering, 'Don't wash it for a week'.

This is a time after the end of the First World War during the Weimar Republic in Germany – a time when there was an audience for local seductresses who performed the function of the modern-day movie star and the contemporary pop star, women who beguiled their audiences with song and entertainment of an evening. As Lola explains to Unraat: 'The men who come here for a few hours ... aah ... respite ... They're far from their homes. They are lonely.' (I, iv). The troupe offers 'simple repose for honest young men who lack the benefit of education'. (Lola, ibid.)

The fascinated professor addresses Lola as 'a lady of some background' as Lola ironically spits in her mascara to moisten it. It is the professor's social status that holds charm for Lola. Her first words to him are: 'It's not often we get a visit from a personage of such status'. (I, iv). Lola doesn't exactly draw in the cream, but her dreams are of an expensive life: 'what I need this minute, is a nice old geezer to come through that door and whisk me off to the Riviera in his Mercedes-Benz.' (I, ix). She wants a 'wallet'. The life of leisure she dreams of is beyond her grasp as the young men like Paul have 'looks' and 'manners' but 'want everything. For nothing.' (Lola, I, x).

Lola is a whore.

> [She strokes her fingers in a gesture of money as she passes [Dieter] – he can have it if he pays for it. (I, vii)

As the schoolboy Paul Eberhardt puts it: 'If you were ever stupid enough to marry a girl like that you'd find yourself out of a job, out of money, out of respect ... just out. [...] Lola's for pleasure.' (I, vi)

The professor is Establishment. As the head of school puts it:

> You are a pillar of this institution, a most valued member of its staff. Your examination results are excellent. You are in charge of the organization of syllabuses. Your conduct in the last twenty-five years that you have been here has always been utterly beyond reproach. (I, viii)

Society's attitude to the professor is reflected in the Headmaster's comment as the professor makes known his decision to marry Lola: 'What a waste'.

The Blue Angel's status increases with the professor's clientele. As Bombler, the manager of The Blue Angel puts it, 'bringing in a Professor night after night raises the tone'. (I, ix)

This is the story of respectability and notoriety. The tale of a small post–World War I town where the veneer of status and respectability forms bourgeois identity. A tale in which the bourgeois betrayal is in the form of a professor of repute who marries the whore who pleasures him. It is the marriage which makes him an outcast – there are other members of the bourgeoisie who frequent The Blue Angel. Our bathetic hero is unaware of the complicity of the economic, juridicial and political institutions – the pillars of society – with the dens of iniquity and it is his idealism and naïvety which lend him a pathos as well as a bathos. It is only after his marriage that Unraat realizes that most of the respected bourgeoisie frequent the establishment which he now owns. For the professor is now trapped in the world of the demi-monde. For a few nights of pleasure he gives up a life of respect and dignity and finds himself 'the owner of [...] a drinking establishment in the docklands area of Hambourg'. (The Judge, II, ii)

Spurned by the bourgeois acquaintances of his past, Unraat turns vicious and seeks to blackmail the most distinguished client of the house: Count von Eberhardt, his ex-pupil Paul's father. As Raat puts it: 'They're all Frauds ... Cheats ... Embezzlers ... all these Pillars of Society'. (II, ii) The character of Raat undergoes a rapid transformation as he turns from being an authoritarian, almost Puritanical pillar of society, to being a blackmailer. It is partly his fascination with Lola, his 'prize' who leaves him desirous of bedecking her with 'jewels such as this city has never seen from every strongroom in Amsterdam ... pearls, ropes of pearls, sapphires, rubies' (II, ii) and partly his realization that he has been outcast for nothing more or less than the other pillars of bourgeois society are guilty of as they all frequent gambling dens and whorehouses albeit secretly. 'Professor Raat is a man who, through his experience of falling in love with a whore, sees the exploitative and hypocritical nature of bourgeois society.'[97]

The money gained disreputably by the once honourable professor is made away with by Dieter and the final mocking of Raat in Dieter's clown suit is the death of an old order. It is a metaphor for the collapsing German economy, the instability that war had wrought on the country and the demise of old hierarchies. Post–World War I Germany comes across as a society of deteriorating moral values as the bourgeoisie and the low life are on par separated merely by materialism and wealth which is held by those who own the means of production. As Raat falls, it is a death of the Germany which was once strong and reputed. Raat's death signals a society in decay and a civilization in crisis. The fall of the one last incorruptible man signals a demise of the old order and a kind of nihilism in the wake of any new structures in a newly fascist Germany.

Aspects of Woman: Dusa, Fish, Stas and Vi
The variety of women in this drama makes it a play on the various identities of queer. The significance of this play stems from the fact that it was the first feminist play to effect a crossover into the mainstream: transferred from the small fringe Hampstead Theatre to the West End Mayfair Theatre. The four women have equal parts and represent aspects of modern woman.

Stas of *Dusa, Fish, Stas and Vi* is another of Gems' portrayals of woman-as-prostitute. In her note on the characters, Gems describes Stas as:

A physiotherapist in a London hospital [who] has a passion for science... for how. The why of life seems to her to be a meaningless question. She is a hostess at night, sleeping with men for high fees. She is discreet, efficient, reliable, and gives good value. Her objective is to save enough money to go to Hawaii to study marine biology.[98]

Perhaps the most unlikely of Gems' whores, Stas spills over from the highly respectable socio-cultural category of physiotherapist to the world with blurred boundaries which encloses the demi-mondaine. Of the four women in the play, it is Stas who is (as Dusa puts it) 'the only one who's not in a mess'. A highly intelligent woman, Stas possesses an objective, scientific, fact-finding mind. Her approach to the others' emotional problems is a philoso-scientific one which uses the knowledge of 'the second law of thermodynamics' interpreted as knowing that there is a 'tendency for things to collapse'. She is caring in an immediate, reliable way, demonstrating the efficiency of the qualified medic in a crisis. Amoral in most senses of the word, Stas is not averse to stealing anything from a fur coat to a bag of nuts, and her ambition to research marine biology would seem to stem more from her desire to make money from a fast developing scientific field rather than a love for any form of life:

Dusa: Oh theories. I'm talking about people.
Stas: (slight pause) We can replicate people now. Did you know that?
Dusa: What?
Stas: And we can cross-breed. A deer with a monkey... an elephant with a cow. Think about it. If you want an animal with rapid maturation... ready to eat in six weeks, with white flesh... and caviare... you've got it. Makes you think, eh? Fifty years from now we shan't need Concorde, we'll all have fins and feathers.
Dusa: Oh, come on.
Stas: True.
Dusa: Oh... well... I don't know anything about it.
Stas: No, that's the trouble with you lot. Back to brown rice and hope for the best. (Act II)

And, as Vi the animal lover dryly puns on Stas's vast collection of furs: 'every fur coat is a stolen coat'.

Dusa, Fish, Stas and Vi are as varied a cross section of women as could ever be thought to live under the same roof. As a group they are diverse, and as aspects of each other they occupy a multiple faceted space which by reason of the *agency* of the female subject in the twentieth century, defies any form of categorization. 'But the four women are also distinct individuals, and each is making a different decision about how she is going to live.'[99] Dusa is a non-working married mother with two children: a traditional role which is clearly one of choice:

> Dusa: I chose it! I knew what I was doing… Why should I have to apologise? I lifted up my tits and went into a beautiful dream… and why not? Seems to me if you're not gay, or battered or one-parent you haven't got it together… (Act I)

Fish is a middle-class woman who 'having considered the inadvertency of her privilege, and the mores of middle class values… has attached herself to a political group on the left.'[100] Vi is an anorexic housebound agoraphobe who has presumably been taken in by Fish who owns the house. The adolescent waif is the youngest of the four and it is Stas, more than the others, who provides her the support she needs to overcome her anorexia nervosa.

Bringing together contemporary women from different backgrounds in an intimate setting, Gems attempts to link them in a sisterhood which, presuming no common ground for their solidarity, nonetheless provides a support system for each. The play is a metaphor for radical feminist ideals which held that women have common experiences and a common cause which binds them through the divisions of class and culture. Toward the end of the play Dusa, Stas and Vi are affirmed as their lives 'work out'; but Fish's unforeseen suicide problematizes the support system of their radical sisterhood. The others fail to detect that Fish is deteriorating to the point where she may relinquish her hold on life as each is wrapped in her immediate concerns: Dusa is ecstatic at the impending safe return of her children, Stas is occupied giving the now recovered Vi a good time, and whilst all three plan a birthday party for Fish, she gives in to despair and takes her life.

Many feminists, including Michelene Wandor, were critical 'of the way it appears to show the only political activist – the socialist feminist – as failing to have any control over her life; she commits suicide.'[101] However, Pam Gems felt that all the characters were 'aspects of the same woman – i.e., any of us – it could have been any of them who committed suicide, a point which an enormous number of people picked up on. There was a political point in making it Fish. The character herself is aware that she is an agent of the revolution. Her middle classness is a cut-off and in one sense it kills her since she feels it's improper for her, the inadvertently privileged woman, to ask for help.'[102] Gems describes Fish as a woman who has the 'natural authority and self confidence of the upper middle classes [who] is seeking to find a supportable, adventurous and equitable way of life with her long standing lover.'[103] In an afterword to the play Gems commented, 'the reason for Fish's decision not to live was the failure of love. The antagonism of the sexes has been painful, an indictment of our age. [...] Fish had tried for a new sharing life with her lover. He didn't want it... he felt better off in a traditional relationship. And she couldn't, wouldn't fight. [...] Fish does not want a fight. Not in the name of love. And without love she dies.'[104]

Whatever be the motives the author ascribes to Fish, the character's obsessive, paranoiac and delusive personality betray an emotionally vulnerable, even immature person despite the intellectual integrity and brave self-confidence displayed in the area of her public life. The opening scene reveals it was Fish who, having chucked the unfaithful Alan, hastily married another man to leave him in a week. By her own admission, she 'should never have done it. *It was only to spite Alan.*' (Act I, emphasis mine). Hardly the way to seek a 'supportable' or 'equitable' life with a lover. Alan finds someone else, and after the failure of her week-old marriage, Fish becomes more and more obsessed with wanting Alan back. Through the play she betrays an overwhelming desire for marriage and children, and Alan. That Fish does want a traditional life is revealed also in her suicide note: 'I wanted so much to sit under a tree with my children and there doesn't seem to be a place for that anymore, and I feel cheated.' (Act II, closing scene). Fish is symptomatic of the kind of first-generation post-liberation woman who, whilst professing herself liberated of traditional values, is programmed to desire, emotionally, the very life-pattern she intellectually rejects. Her leftist politics can offer no solace, as her emotional needs are in severe conflict with her active intellectual socio-political life; this leads to a breakdown of her personality into the obsessive and paranoid state she displays toward the end of the play. This conflict seems to be the cause of her suicide rather than a simplistic loss of love.

Dusa's fate seems to be similar: having opted for the traditional role she is abandoned by a husband she still loves. Neither Fish nor Dusa can win, and Fish's suicide note is telling in its implications of the emotional position of women at a time when their gender role was (and still remains) largely unresolved. 'My loves, what are we to do? We won't do as they want anymore, and they hate it. What are we to do?' (Act II)

Just as Fish is not a stereotype, nor is Dusa. 'She is not overtly "motherly" because she has two children, i.e., she is not soppy, or pea-brained or henlike. She *is* split, displaying the angst and the particular vulnerability of the breeding bitch; also the restless boredom.'[105] Gems alludes more than once to the 'breeding bitch' in her plays; this seems to be the type of woman who enjoys creating in an almost addictive fashion. As Dusa explains: 'I wish I were a cat or a horse. I'd have one a year. Your body wants to go on. Once it's got the hang of it.' (Act I). In *Loving Women* Frank describes Crystal as 'restless': 'She doesn't know it but what she really wants is a child every other year. That's what her body wants. They're all breeders, the women in her family. Insatiable.' (Act II). Dusa, unlike Crystal, doesn't work; and when her husband takes the children away and leaves she is left without her economic and emotional lifeline. Rendered powerless and helpless Dusa is ironically saved by Stas's ill-gotten gains which she is encouraged to steal, which allows her the freedom to trace the whereabouts of her children. 'Breeding' is what Dusa does, and of course for this she needs the economic support of her husband. But like the other characters of the play, Dusa is not a 'type' but an aspect of the contemporary identity the four women symbolise. It is in Crystal of *Loving Women* that we find a crystallization of economic independence, sensuous sexuality and woman's creative biological powers which are transmuted into woman-power at its most potent in the contemporary world.

The Split Gestus of Woman: Loving Women

Crystal is another portrait of the contemporary mother as was Dusa in *Dusa, Fish, Stas and Vi*. Crystal's is however a working-class portrait stretching the queer identity of gender once more into a class category. Again, Gems has her occupying several categories at once so it is difficult to label her as either mother, wife, working woman, or indeed sex symbol. It seems too facile to name her as merely 'a dizzy working-class blonde ... an uneducated sex-pot',[106] 'sex-crazy Crystal'.[107] These definitions undoubtedly point to the masculist bias of the reviewers, and point also to the iconic representation of the character (which would in turn activate masculist critiques). Crystal's development through the play reveals the serious materialism of the 1980s[108], but equally, it is a sketch of the triumph of the working classes as they achieve social mobility. At the opening of the play she seems the stereotype of a sexy, dim-witted blonde whom Frank chooses to marry over serious-thinking Susannah. Gems seems to satirise the male psyche by juxtaposing two, apparently opposite, kinds of women: the stereotypes of the 'bimbo' and the 'intelligent thinking woman' where, like Alan of *Dusa, Fish, Stas and Vi* Frank makes a traditional patriarchal choice opting for 'a delicious body – and home cooking.'[109] Act I is devoted to the two women acting as a foil to each other: Crystal demonstrating a vitality and freshness to Susannah's serious level-headedness. Crystal dismisses Susannah's 'lot' as 'liberated' – which they are. They 'put [Crystal] off':

Crystal: I thought he was going to bring out the manual – Christ, what are they after, good marks or something?

Susannah: You like the man to take the lead?

Crystal: Sure … within reason. Tell you one thing, your lot's never going to be up for rape. (I, i)

It is Susannah who had asked Crystal to nurse Frank through his illness since she was too busy working – the last thing she expected was for Frank (whom she had been with for five years) to marry what seems to be a clearly unsuitable Crystal. She confronts Frank after the wedding with bitter sarcasm:

Susannah: Well, since I'm here, you might as well fill me in. Like, why you did it.
(He doesn't answer)
Was it the breakdown?
(He looks nervous that Crystal might hear)
Well, what? Some kind of gesture … direct-action consciousness raising? Or did you just fall for nursey? (I, ii)

But Frank has changed. Disillusioned with communist ideals he now works as a schoolteacher and is a member of the Labour Party. And he more than loves his wife: he is mesmerized by her sensuality and beauty. However, he enjoys Susannah's conversation and stimulating intellect. She sums him up acidly and perhaps quite accurately:

Frank: I don't know anything. Except her. (Pause) I read to her. In the evenings. We're reading Lord Jim at the moment. Remember the opening, where he goes on about Jim's job as a tout for a ship's chandler?

Susannah: What?

Frank: After a couple of pages describing the tattiness of a tout's life he ends up … 'a beautiful and humane occupation'. Irony. She liked that. She got it. (Pause)

Susannah: You pompous renegade. You bloody social-democrat do-gooder.

Frank: It's real. I feel real.

Susannah: Well, good luck to you. (She picks up her bag.) What's she like in bed?
Frank: A goer. I have trouble keeping up.

Susannah: I notice she does all the cooking and shopping, all the work. What's in it for her?

Frank: She wants a husband, children. She's not after the world.

Susannah: She'd better be, or she'll end up like your Mum and mine ... vicious.
You bloody exploitative shit. I hope it rots off. (She leaves). (I, ii)

But as the scene closes on Frank and Crystal they seem genuinely happy:

Crystal:	She gone?
	(He nods)
	Jesus.
	(He doesn't reply. She contemplates him)
	I had a shower.
Frank:	Oh?
Crystal:	Smell me.
Frank:	(grabbing her and burying his face): Mmmmmm ...
Crystal:	Guess what it is ... no, you got to guess ...
Frank:	It's called 'Expensive'.
Crystal:	You ain't seen nothing.
(laughing)	(She drops the dressing gown. She is wearing very little, but it is sensational.)
Frank:	Christ!
Crystal:	Thought I'd better do something.
Frank:	No need.
Crystal:	Really?
Frank:	Look, it's old history.
Crystal:	I started to feel like, you know, a fucking gooseberry in me own place.
Frank:	Finished. Over.
Crystal:	Right. Well ... in that case ...
	(She sits on his lap, legs astride)
Frank:	Here, what about my dinner?
Crystal:	It'll keep. (She kisses him)
Frank:	I'm a hungry man.
Crystal:	I know. (kisses him)
	I've made allowances. (Kisses him)
	Last course first tonight ...
	(They embrace as lights go to black). (I, ii)

Act I ends on Crystal's intense insecurity about Susannah. Act II opens in 1984 to reverse the tables. Ten years have passed and Crystal is a successful West End hairstylist who 'pulls a fortune'. She has successfully mothered two children, a boy and a girl; looks sensational and well-maintained, and supports her family practically single-handedly. Frank offers a tribute to her fertile and sexual body in terms one would ascribe to a goddess: 'She has such a body ... breasts ... contours ... valleys ... all – alive! It's a crime to clothe her ... she should be decked with flowers and worshipped. I'm a mere mortal. I deprive her. So she takes it out of me.' (II)

These two women dis-play together the central gestus of post-liberation 'woman': as two separate beings they serve to re-present the needs and desires of the male. Sensuality and sexuality is divided from intellect, both of which the man desires: however, intellect is something he can derive from platonic friendships and isn't something he necessarily marries. Crystal seems to have the best of all possible worlds: Frank even ignores her promiscuity as long as she doesn't bring it home with her. The economic power Crystal wields has, in effect, reversed the power nexus between the sexes: and combined with the sexual power she has over Frank, Crystal occupies the power-position that generations of men have had over their wives. Even though Frank does leave in the end, Crystal is complacent: she knows he will be back. And if he doesn't: 'Sod him! Who needs him!' she says dismissively. Frank, one suspects, would not have put up with Crystal's sexual forays if not for the freedom her earnings offered him to pursue the path he desires:

Susannah: How's the job?
Frank: I'm supply teaching at the moment.
Susannah: Are you? I had you all dug in as senior history master. You look pretty busy. (She picks up a pamphlet).
Frank: Socialist Combination. I've thrown my lot in, now that it's highly unfashionable.
           (They laugh)
Susannah: And what about freedom from party dogma?
Frank: Ah. Freedom. Plenty of that about. Freedom to sink. To go to hell. Opportunities for boys to train as butlers – I'm not kidding, there was a programme on television.
Susannah: What about women?
Frank: Unemployment hasn't helped. The scene's changed since you left.
Susannah: Oh, how?
Frank: More polarized, I think.
           I'll run you down to Greenham.
Susannah: Already been. So, you're active?
Frank: Full-time from next month.
Susannah: You're giving up teaching? Completely?
(surprised)

Frank: I'll miss it.
(nods)
Susannah: Can you afford to?
Frank: Just about. (He shrugs) Crystal pulls a fortune. (II)

Susannah the idealist do-gooder has returned from her years in Bolivia with regrets about her work, about having lost Frank, about the Pill which promised freedom to women but only seemed to delay the choice of motherhood until it was too late:

Susannah: I've gone over and over it in my mind. I should have been there. When you were ill. I realise that now.
Frank: I wasn't myself.
Susannah: I should have been there. That bloody project – God, we were so intense! We were going to change the world. Hah.
Frank: I know.
Susannah: I thought we were indissoluble. Mistake number one. We were so in step … at least that's what I thought. That fucking Pill.
Frank: What?
Susannah: If it weren't for the Pill I'd have been pregnant three times over, the way we went at it.
            […]
            God, the agony of choice! (She groans) I mean! There's never a good time to have a baby, if you can afford it you're too old, and who needs Marmite sandwiches and little morons for ten years when you're just getting your head together – God, How I envy Crystal! (II)

Susannah returns to want the very things Crystal has: Frank, healthy children, a home, a family. Crystal's solution of a three-pronged communal arrangement appeals to Susannah – it would mean that the children would have their parents, Susannah would have Frank, while Crystal would be free to enjoy the active sexual life she seems to need. The play ends much as Churchill would end *Traps* (1977) and *Cloud Nine* (1979) – with an attempt at communal living. As Adrienne Rich remarked in a reflection on the changing institution of family in the late twentieth century: 'To seek visions, to dream dreams, is essential, and it is also essential to try new ways of living, to make room for serious experimentation, to respect the effort even where it fails.'[110] An experiment with communal living here is different from the triadic arrangement in *Aunt Mary*, below, as this affords Crystal the space for the sexual freedom she needs. However, this attempt also contests the nuclear family bringing the threesome and their children into a queer subcultural space.

In the 1990s Gems has focussed on a male protagonist – the English artist Stanley Spencer in *Stanley* (1996). This may seem a divergence from her women-centred plays but is in keeping with her integrationist ideology. In the gamut of her work, however, Gems has given the prototypic straw women many lives and has demonstrated an ability to bring woman out from behind the veil of stereotypes infusing woman with a life long denied. In dramaturgical and theatrical terms Gems, 'the grande dame of British Theatre'[111] has retrieved woman and shattered the prototypical stereotype much as a prism shatters light revealing a bright and radiant rainbow of plurality. She has revealed the queer subcultural identity of western woman in all its variety.

NOTES

1. Western woman has been collectively elided from discourse which has always been constituted as a male space. This is a starkly different history to that of the Indian woman who contributed to the earliest philosophical work, the *Rg-veda* (c. 1500 BCE) and was also free to write poetry and literature from earliest recorded history. See Dimple Godiwala, 'The Sacred and the Feminine: Indian women poets writing since 600 BCE' in *LinQ*, summer 2005, forthcoming.

2. S. Harding, 'Reinventing Ourselves as Other', in L. Kauffman, ed., *American Feminist Thought at Century's End - A Reader*, Blackwell, 1993, p.156.

3. The historical Queen Christina is reported to have said this. All historical references to Christina are from Betty Millan, *Monstrous Regiment: Women Rulers in Men's Worlds*, The Kensal Press, 1982, pp.168-181.

4. Marjorie Garber, *Vice Versa: Bisexuality and the Eroticism of Everyday Life*, Hamish Hamilton, 1995, p.70.

5. Hélène Cixous, 'The Laugh of the Medusa', in *New French Feminisms*, eds. Elaine Marks and Isabelle de Courtivron, Harvester, 1980.

6. Pam Gems in 'Spare Rib', September 1977. My emphasis.

7. See Roland Barthes, *Mythologies* [1957], trans. Jonathan Cape, 1972, Vintage, 1993, pp.109–159; and the later *Image - Music - Text*, Fontana Press, 1977, p.165.

8. Cf *Mythologies*, p.128.

9. *Mythologies*, p. 127.

10. *Mythologies*, p. 123.

11. Cf *Mythologies*, pp. 120–122.

12. There are a group of feminists who oppose the writing of Herstory. e.g., Christina Crosby, in *The Ends of History: Victorians and 'The Woman Question'* insists that revealing women where there had been only men is still to occupy the space of formation of the discourse of history; that such herstoricizing would reveal 'the truth' about women's lives just as history had purported to about man's identity (that women have always occupied the space of the

Other); and thirdly, women would be conceptualized as a unified category of similar individuals with similar experiences, where differences would be neglected. Diane Elam counters by asserting that *'her-story is not just one story'* (authorial emphasis). As Cixous put it in *The Newly Born Woman*, there are always several [herstories] underway at once. The diversity and plurality of herstories must then be acknowledged and accounted for. Anti-herstorians must also recognize that history can be an integrated whole only if the achievements – both personal and political – of both genders are recorded. Most importantly, feminists who work within a recognized canonical/ patriarchal discourse destabilize the bounds of that discourse by demanding ideological accommodation within it. Herstoricizing thus *breaks the bounds* of his-tory by reformulating it. Diane Elam, *Feminism and Deconstruction: Ms. en Abyme*, Routledge, 1994, p.37.Christina Crosby, *The Ends of History: Victorians and 'The Woman Question'*, Routledge, 1991, p. 153. Quoted in Elam, op. cit.Hélène Cixous, *The Newly Born Woman*, (*La Jeune Née*), co-written with Catherine Clèment, pub. 1975, trans. Betsy Wing, University of Minnesota Press, 1986. p.160.

13. *e.g.*, The Women's Theatre Group and Elaine Feinstein's *Lear's Daughters* (1987).

14. *Feminism and Deconstruction*, p.67.

15. Quoted in 'The Plays of Pam Gems' in *British and Irish Drama*, p.192.

16. *Feminism and Deconstruction*, pp. 42–43.

17. Judith Butler, *Bodies That Matter: On the Discursive Limits of Sex*, Routledge, 1993.

18. *Bodies That Matter*. See also her earlier *Gender Trouble: Feminism and the Subversion of Identity*, Routledge, 1990. The heterosexual matrix might be defined as the discursive field of normativity which prescribes heterosexuality as a regulatory ideal. The heterosexual matrix would be imbricated within the patriarchal field of discursivity which activates the patriarchal perceptual screens through which subjects view the world.

19. *Bodies That Matter*.

20. *Gender Trouble,* pp.142–143.

21. This dialectical movement runs through everything Hegel wrote: that every condition of thought or of things leads irresistibly to its opposite, and then (ideally) unites with it to form a higher or more complex whole. It is an old thought, foreshadowed by Empedocles, and embodied in the 'golden mean' of Aristotle who wrote 'the knowledge of opposites is one'. Will Durant, *The Story of Philosophy*, Washington Square Press, [1926] 1953, pp.272, 292ff.

22. *Feminism and Deconstruction*, p.75.

23. *Gender Trouble*, pp.144–145. My emphasis.

24. Jacques Derrida, 'White Mythology' (1971), in *Margins of Philosophy*, trans. Alan Bass, Chicago: Chicago University Press, 1982, pp.213–214. Undoubtedly, Derrida here is not just referring to gender as the exergue of western philosophy, but almost certainly the knowledge of the colonized and racial Other. The argument, however, is pertinent to the construction of western philosophy which relegates gendered knowledge to an exergue.

25. Just as Christina's identity was 'forced into materialization' by her patriarch's decision to rear her as a man, so was Garbo formulated by the Garbo experts: director, photographer, costume expert, scriptwriter. The censors similarly played a role in demanding any 'tinge of lesbianism' be underplayed. See: *Queen Christina*, Marcia Landy and Amy Villarejo, British Film Institute, 1995. Cited as *Queen Christina*, BFI publication.

26. *Queen Christina*, BFI publication, p.22.

27. Monstrous Regiment.

28. *Carry On, Understudies*, p.164.

29. *Queen Christina*, BFI publication.

30. Adrienne Rich, *Of Woman Born: Motherhood as Experience and Institution*, first published, USA: 1976; UK Virago 1977, p.235.

31. *Carry On*, p. 149.

32. For usurping the feminine, see Butler's interpretation of Foucault's reading of Herculine Barbin. *Gender Trouble*, pp.99-101.

33. *Gender Trouble*, p.111.

34. Parker Tyler, quoted in *Gender Trouble*, p.128.

35. *The Newly Born Woman*, p.85.

36. *The Newly Born Woman*, p.85.

37. *The Newly Born Woman*, pp.84–85.

38. *Gender Trouble*, p.93.

39. *Gender Trouble*, p.93.

40. *Gender Trouble*, p.93.

41. *Gender Trouble*, p.96.

42. *The Newly Born Woman*, p.85.

43. *The Newly Born Woman*, p.88.

44. See Hélène Cixous and Catherine Clément, 'Sorties: Out and Out: Attacks/ Ways Out/ Forays', in *The Newly Born Woman*, [*La Jeune Née*, 1975], trans. Betsy Wing, University of Minnesota Press, 1986, p.63.

45. *The Newly Born Woman*, p.65.

46. *The Newly Born Woman*, p.65

47. *The Newly Born Woman*, p.8.

48. *The Newly Born Woman*, pp.68–69.

49. *The Newly Born Woman*, p.67.

50. Letter to the author from Jonathan Gems, 18 April 2004.

51. Gems in the Foreword to the play. In the original draft sent to author, 2001.

52. Geoffrey Chaucer, 'General Prologue', *The Canterbury Tales*, in *The Riverside Chaucer*, Oxford University Press, 1988, p.28.

53. See Dimple Godiwala, *Breaking the Bounds: British Feminist Dramatists Writing in the Mainstream since c. 1980*, Peter Lang, 2003, part II, chapter II.

54. Lyn Gardner, 'Precious Gems', *Plays and Players*, April 1985, p.13.

55. Simone de Beauvoir, *The Second Sex* (*Le Deuxième Sexe*, 1949), trans. and ed., H. M. Parshley, Jonathan Cape, 1953, reprt. Penguin 1983. Hereafter cited in the text as TSS followed by page number.

56. See Stella Sandford, 'Contingent Ontologies: Sex, gender and 'woman' in Simone de Beauvoir and Judith Butler', *Radical Philosophy*, No.97, September/October 1999, pp.18–29.

57. *Feminism and Deconstruction*, p.37.

58. *The Newly Born Woman*, p.160.

59. Nancy Cotton, *Woman Playwrights in England c.1363–1750*, New Jersey, London and Toronto: Associated University Presses, 1980, p.64.

60. Katherine Worth, 'Images of Women in Modern English Theatre', in Enoch Brater, ed. *Feminine Focus: The New Women Playwrights*, Oxford University Press, 1989, p.10.

61. George Bernard Shaw, Preface to *Mrs.Warren's Profession* in *Plays Unpleasant*.

62. Margaret Llewellyn-Jones, 'Claiming a Space: 1969–78' in *British and Irish Women Dramatists since 1958*, ed. Trevor R. Griffiths and Margaret Llewellyn-Jones, Oxford University Press, 1993, p.36.

63. Roland Barthes, 'The Lady of the Camellias' in *Mythologies*, pp.103–105.

64. *Mythologies*, pp.103–105.

65. *British and Irish Women Dramatists*, p.36.

66. *Mythologies*, p.104.

67. *Mythologies*, p.104.

68. *British and Irish Women Dramatists*, p.37.

69. *British and Irish Women Dramatists*, p.37.

70. *British and Irish Women Dramatists*, p.37.

71. James Redmond, '"If the salt has lost his savour": Some "useful" plays in and out of context on the London stage', in *The Play out of Context: Transferring Plays from Culture to Culture*, eds. Hanna Scolnicov and Peter Holland, Cambridge University Press, 1989, p.73.

72. *British and Irish Women Dramatists*, p.37.

73. Heidi Stephenson and Natasha Langridge, *Rage and Reason: Women Playwrights on Playwriting*, Methuen, 1997, p.91.

74. *Carry On*, p.162.

75. Pauline Peters, *The Sunday Times*, 3 February 1980.

76. *Carry On*, p.163.

77. Jack Tinker, *The Daily Mail*, 14 December 1993.

78. *Legends of the Twentieth Century: Edith Piaf*, EMI CD.

79. See Pam Gems' introduction to *Marlene*, Oberon Books, 1998.

80. However, the evocation of myth by the citation of an overused fragment takes time. Gems' *Piaf* is too young in audience memory and production history for this statement to be valid

at this moment in time. To evoke Edith Piaf, however, a few strains of '*Je ne regrette rien*' would be enough.

81. Michael Billington in *The Guardian*, 15 December 1993.

82. Sheridan Morley in *The Spectator*, 1 January 1994.

83. Benedict Nightingale in *The Times*, 15 December 1993.

84. Louise Doughty in *The Mail on Sunday*, 19 December 1993.

85. Sheridan Morley in *The Spectator*, 1 January 1994

86. Clive Hirschhorn in *Sunday Express*, 19 December 1993.

87. Louise Doughty in *The Mail on Sunday*, 19 December 1993.

88. Irving Wardle in *The Independent*, 19 December 1993.

89. Jane Lapotaire, comments Pam Gems, was well cast as Piaf. 'The actress as famous as Gielgud for her tongue – when accosted by a friend as she came out of the Brompton Oratory [she said]: 'Fuck off, can't you see I'm in a state of fucking blues?' Letter to the author from Pam Gems, 8 November 2000.

90. Benedict Nightingale in *The Times*, 15 December 1993.

91. Irving Wardle in *The Independent*, 19 December 1993.

92. Charles Spencer in *The Daily Telegraph*, 15 December 1993.

93. Sue-Ellen Case, *Feminist Theatre*, Macmillan, 1988.

94. Letter to the author from Jonathan Gems, 18 April 2004.

95. Jonathan Gems points out that this play was entirely based on the novel, which is very different from the film. However, Trevor Nunn's production 'was probably influenced by the film.' Letter to the author from Jonathan Gems, 18 April 2004.

96. Introduction to *Marlene,* Oberon, 1998.

97. Jonathan Gems in a letter to the author, 18 April 2004.

98. Pam Gems, 'Notes on the Characters' in *Plays by Women: Volume I*, ed., Michelene Wandor, Methuen, 1983.

99. Michelene Wandor, 'Women are the uncharted territory', Interview with Pam Gems in *Spare Rib*, September 1977, p.13.

100. Pam Gems, 'Notes on the Characters' in *Plays by Women: Volume I*, ed., Michelene Wandor, Methuen, 1983.

101. Michelene Wandor, 'Women are the uncharted territory', Interview with Pam Gems in *Spare Rib*, September 1977, p.13.

102. Pam Gems, 'Women are the uncharted territory', Interview with Pam Gems in *Spare Rib*, September 1977, p.13.

103. Pam Gems, 'Notes on the Characters' in *Plays by Women: Volume I*, ed., Michelene Wandor, Methuen, 1983.

104. Pam Gems, Afterword, in *Plays by Women: Volume I*, ed., Michelene Wandor, Methuen, 1983.

105. Pam Gems, 'Notes on the Characters' in *Plays by Women: Volume I*, ed., Michelene Wandor, Methuen, 1983.

106. John Barber in *The Daily Telegraph*, 2 February 1984.

107. Michael Ratcliffe in *The Observer*, 5 February 1984.

108. Cf. Caryl Churchill's *Top Girls*.

109. John Barber in *The Daily Telegraph*, 2 February 1984.

110. Adrienne Rich, *Of Woman Born: Motherhood as Experience and Institution*, first published USA, 1976; Britain: Virago, 1977, p.282.

111. In Lyn Gardner's phrase, quoted in 'The Plays of Pam Gems' in *British and Irish Drama*, p.190.

3

OF STRAIGHT AND GAY MEN: MASCULINITIES IN CRISIS

Not content to portray the multiple facets of contemporary woman, Gems art turns toward 'men' in all their guises: straight, gay, transsexual, transgendered. She writes about Stanley Spencer, the British artist and his life and loves; Garibaldi, the Maker of modern Italy; Freud's student and critic Franz Perls and, in *Aunt Mary*, she portrays transgendered characters who seek a new way of existence.

AUNT MARY: THE DIALECTICS OF DESIRE

> ... to take sex out of transvestism is like taking music out of opera.
> — *H. Benjamin*, The Transsexual Phenomenon 1

> It is not the reader's "person" that is necessary to me, it is this site: the possibility of a dialectics of desire, of an *unpredictability* of bliss: the bets are not placed, there can still be a game. — *Roland Barthes*, The Pleasure of the Text

To say that *Aunt Mary* is a play about three gay people would be misleading. The transgendered identities and triadic domestic arrangements of this 1982 drama challenge the notions of traditionally gendered space and the nuclear family. Pam Gems is on the pulse of the gender theorizing of the 1990s well before it happened:

she anticipates the transgendered spaces of gay and queer theory in the early 1980s when fledgling lesbian theory had not given way to queer and gay theorizing quite yet. Gender here is set against a heterogeneous social background to give us 'Aunt' Mary, a middle-aged gay man, Muriel, a bisexual middle-aged woman and, Cyst, an aging transvestite male, who star in this three-pronged drama about love, gender and sexual relationships, privacy and capitalist materialism. When Alison who works for a media mogul wants to take the eminently saleable lives of this threesome into the glare of the public eye of television, they refuse to give up the privacy of their provincial lives. Indeed, the subtitle of the play is *Scenes from Provincial Life* making the metadramatic statement of enacting in performance exactly what Alison the media person wants: putting the three transgendered people into the frame of the stage and bringing into confrontation the difference from the normative in contemporary Britain. This is a performance of the identity of drag and queer framed by a play: the shifting space in which the identities of the players locate themselves is a study in the psychology of transgendering, transvestitism and transsexualism, which perform versions of a variously gay identity space.

As Jonathan Gems sees it: '[T]he play is [also] about art, artists and the dangerous relationship between art and the media which exploits and "rewards" it. Too much success for the artist is a poisoned chalice. Aunt Mary and Cyst are prolific authors who avoid the damage of success by writing under a plethora of pseudonyms. But their cover is blown by the poet whose girlfriend is a television arts producer… whose ambition almost destroys them. We see here the ambivalent attitude of "management" for the artist. Management, by its nature, is parasitical on the artist – yet it despises and ultimately seeks to destroy the artist. […] As Sting said in an interview: "If it's good for the music business, it's bad for music."'[2]

The play avoids the easy exclusions that the new identity positions place on people named gay, bisexual, lesbian, transvestite and transsexual (TV/TSS). As Alan Sinfield theorizes, the notion of the subject as defined by these, albeit fairly new, cultural terms, is a constraint. He notes that these terms may prove a hindrance to activists and analysts rather than an aid.[3] Although the term 'transgender' is currently used to encompass the subjective identities of all TVs and TSS, Jay Prosser explains that 'transgender' was used initially to denote a stronger commitment to living as a woman than 'transvestite' or 'cross-dresser', and without the implications of sexuality in 'transsexual'.[4]

Cyst, Mary and Muriel defy definitions of constraint through this play by occupying different positions within exclusivity and difference. Although certain behaviours sound conventional in the play such as cross-dressing (Cyst enters from within, wearing a half-made dress. Mary follows, tape measure round neck. (Scene iv), so-called 'effeminate behaviour' within the literary space of their café, and the manufactured masculinity apparent in Mary's appearance in trousers with a cigar, these temper gay behaviour to be socially acceptable in the triad of wo/men.

Sinfield and other western metropolitan gay theorists' 1990s discovery via Other (mainly Eastern) cultures[5] that there are 'radically different ways in which people can conceive their subjectivity and focus their desire' is an issue prefigured by Pam Gems in *Aunt Mary* by nearly a decade.

The play rescues these behaviours from the traditional negative and prejudiced forms by which they have been addressed. Transvestism (TV) and transsexualism (TSS) were traditionally diagnostic terms for categories of mental disorders.[6] Later, in 'self theory' which posits the self as a hypothetical construct, the concepts of identity, gender identity and cross-gender identity are conceptualized by Richard F. Docter as 'subsystems of the self'. Docter et al. hypothesize that the self has a capacity to 'share control, and even [...] be "overthrown" by subordinate units of the self.'[7] One approach to transvestism is the *intrapsychic/psychodynamic model*. According to R. F. Docter, the best of psychoanalytic models of transvestism 'describe this as a disorder of the self stemming from major difficulties in early object relations. Women's clothing are said to be symbolic ties with the mother and to serve as transitional objects providing security and anxiety reduction.' Docter opines that 'this theory seems more in harmony with the developmental behaviour of a transvestite than the earlier "phallic woman" model that drew mainly on castration anxiety and the oedipal complex as explanatory theses.' The *developmental/ learning model* 'attempts to explain transvestism and transsexualism based on the principles of learning and the process of socialization. The idea is that these behaviours are acquired through classical conditioning, operant conditioning, and model[l]ing and imitation, just as are so many other behaviours.' Since the different models explaining TV and TSS conflict with each other, Docter devises four thematic constructs in order to view these behaviours conceptually. He seems to ignore the *biological* or *medical model* entirely and favours developmental psychology. The four constructs are: *sexual arousal* and sexual excitement at cross-dressing; the *pleasure* associated with cross-dressing in the sense of its mood-altering power; *sexual scripts* which guide complex behaviour; and *cross-gender identity* which is switched on and off by the act of cross-dressing.[8]

There seem to be two main explanations for transvestism: one is that it is a means for achieving sexual pleasure and arousal; the second is that transvestism is part of a personality struggle stemming from trauma and conflict. Docter aims to go beyond these two theories to question 'how identity and gender identity are formed, how arousal and pleasure are generated, how sexual scripts are learned and rehearsed, and how intense envy and fear of women may contribute to becoming a transvestite.'[9]

It does seem that even contemporary analysts see transgendered behaviour as abnormal or problem behaviour though their terminology is couched in a more progressive and acceptable language of analysis. The formation of gender and sexual identity, the generation of pleasure and the playing out of sexual scripts are not peculiar to transgendered people, and these can be as differently and variously constructed and enacted as there are gender and sexual identities. In the play we see the three transgendered wo/men play out these various sexual scripts. The female impersonator in Aunt Mary is 'Cyst'. Her favourite impersonation is the character of Blanche DuBois, a favourite of the cross-dressing community, perhaps because in *A Streetcar Named Desire*[10] she symbolises the dichotomy between inner and outer self, the core of self and the facade of self, lending the cross-dresser the 'magic' of Blanche's outward coy femininity masking the 'realism' of the impersonating male self. Here we see the self has a capacity to share control, and even be 'overthrown' by subordinate units of the self: transsexualism.

> I don't want realism. [...] I'll tell you what I want. Magic! Yes, yes, magic! I try to give that to people. I misrepresent things to them. I don't tell the truth. I tell what *ought* to be truth. And if that is sinful, then let me be damned for it! – *Don't turn the light on!* (Blanche in *A Streetcar Named Desire*, p. 204)

Cyst hates the real light of day as does Blanche, perfectly in character and also quite apt psychologically as she is an agoraphobe who never leaves the environs of the house and the garden. Cyst enjoys women's clothing which serves as a transitional object providing security and anxiety reduction. Cyst is the impersonating wench.

The wench as played by male impersonators on the stage is traced by Laurence Senelick to the burlesque of *La Dame aux Camélias* (or *Camille* as it is known in the United States) which has Sam and Julius re-creating Dumas' tragedy. Senelick also traces the interweaving of the psychology of race relations with the sexual desire, 'particularly in such manifestations as dominance and submission, exoticism and the attraction of opposites.' He traces the later genre where 'men frankly portrayed lovely white women' to Charles du Val, a mid-Victorian performer. However, the extravagant wardrobes, close male partnership and prolonged bachelorhood, as deeply suspect as they are to the modern theatre historian, did not plunge the performers into disrepute: 'no breath of homosexual scandal touched [the] unmarried female impersonators of the minstrel stage. They were actors, and that explained everything.'[11]

Richard Howard's preface to Roland Barthes' *The Pleasure of the Text* deconstructs English amorous discourse as 'coarse or clinical'. '[B]y tradition our words for our pleasures, even for the most intimate parts of our bodies where we may take those pleasures, come awkwardly [if] they come at all. So that if we wish to speak of the kind of pleasure we take – the supreme pleasure, say, associated with sexuality at its most abrupt and ruthless pitch [bisexual, gay, TV/TSS] – we lack. [...] [W]e lack *jouissance* and *jouir*.' Howard reminds us that Sterne [*The Life and Opinions of Tristram Shandy* 1759–1767] said, 'they order this matter so much better in France.'[12]

Interestingly, or perhaps predictably, today's amorous discourse in England is constituted by the new gay, queer and trans-gender studies writings and performance. Sex and sexuality, repressed in the heterosexual closet, come out in an abundant *jouir* as well as possess a *jouissance* beyond the 'phallus' (the system) in the matrix of these performative and analytic discourses.

Cyst can also be seen as trans-gendered, which Alan Sinfield recognizes as a *gender* identity rather than a sub-category of sexual identity. Kenneth Marlowe defines two kinds of homosexuals: the 'effeminate' and the 'masculine'. '[I]t is paternal rejection of the "sissy" that makes the boy homosexual: sexuality is consequent upon gender attributes.'[13] Sinfield traces the historical fact that the notion of trans-gendered identity has always existed: 'the kind of gay man whose effeminacy was tantamount to trans-gender [was always] visible'. Recognizing Quentin Crisp as trans-gendered, he is defined thus by his very words: the kind of persons who 'must, with every breath they draw, with every step they take, demonstrate that they are feminine'.[14] The kind of person who is continually 'propositioned, harassed and beaten by total strangers. Employers and the army reject him on sight'.[15]

Cyst may also be played as a hermaphrodite or by a transsexual actor as in Kate Bornstein's 1988 enaction of Herculine Barbin, Michel Foucault's case study. Barbin's interstitial position between the sexes is voiced by Bornstein the transsexual actor who identifies with 'hir':

> [T]he journey I want to portray is, did [Barbin] really have to be a he or a she? Was he really some other gender that was trying to survive? And that's the way I feel

myself ... I certainly don't feel I'm a man, and many times I question whether I'm a woman. I laugh at a world that permits me to be only one or the other.[16]

Barbin's memoirs were written as a study of what Michel Foucault saw as the essentialist position of the '*true* sex'.

Do we *truly* need a *true* sex? With a persistence that borders on stubbornness, modern Western societies have answered in the affirmative. They have obstinately brought into play this question of a "true" sex in an order of things where one might have imagined that all that counted was the reality of the body and the intensity of its pleasures.[17]

Foucault brings into question the persistence of the western practice of perceiving the sexes as a duality. '[I]t was a very long time before the postulate that a hermaphrodite must have a sex – a single, true sex – was formulated.' Sexuality for Foucault was always constructed within matrices of power as Butler reminds us.[18] In the play we have Cyst as an indefinable space in the text, the gay cross-dressed actor or indeed a transsexual actor who responds to Aunt Mary's masculinity but also provides a female/feminine power of hir own. They function in a two-pronged matrix of power relations as they finally include Muriel into a triadic domesticity which is, in a subversion of the Deleuzean Oedipal-nuclear triad, a benign power relation. In a metadramatic twist we see the characters of Cyst and Mary 'perform' for us, as they reject in a final gesture the beckoning materialist temptation of media celebrity and exposure. They are not, in the play, public impersonators but privately, a gay couple leading a 'provincial life'. As in *Franz into April* (below) their life unfolds in a theatrical space, as the theatre doubles as a private (confessional) and public (performative) space which contains the flows of their desires. Susan Carlson,[19] whilst admitting that this play, like *Camille*, 'reinterprets theatre structures so that the disproportionate power of conclusions works for, not against, women and others on the margin of society', fails to recognise the enormous disruptive power of this play in terms of the social constructions of gender and sexuality. Describing it as a 'comic, male-centred [sic], off-beat stage failure', Carlson misses the metaphors which formulate the *agency* of the sexually gendered subject/s in the making of non-normative choices of self-construction[20] in the face of conventionally pre-determined modes of being. What does it mean for the audience that the subjects of the play 'cite' the law (nominals, dress codes, behaviour etc.) to produce it differently? That the play dis-plays that gender performativity is 'not a singular "act"', that it is 'always a reiteration of a norm or set of norms [...] to the extent that it acquires an act-like status [which] conceals or dissimulates the convention of which it is a repetition' means that citing the normative law to produce it differently is 'to "cite" the law in order to reiterate and coopt its power, to expose the heterosexual matrix and to displace the effect of its necessity'. The citational politics of queerness becomes an enabling disruption which re-works and resignifies the abjection of homosexuality into defiance and legitimacy.[21] Cross-dressing, for example, makes tangible the appearance of the 'naturalness' of gender, as the self-consciousness of the cross-dresser, the use of exaggeration and parody and posturing all reveal the artifice of gender and sexuality.

An understanding of Gilles Deleuze and Félix Guattari's theory in *Anti-Oedipus: Capitalism and Schizophrenia* sheds light on the central gestus of this play. The triadic arrangement which closes the play is a line of flight from heteronormative institutions of repression; it is also a flight from gay sexual constraints by the acceptance of bi-sexuality, deemed 'natural' by some essentialist theorists such as Hélène Cixous. The triadic union of male impersonator-as-woman, a gay man and a woman in a legitimized marriage is the triadic answer to Deleuze's critique of the nuclear family (and capitalism) as source and the core of the ills of capitalism, indeed of all repression. It is also a response to the repressed feminine of the male-male bonding of conventional gay sexuality. It is the realization of 'freedom in difference and through differentiation, the principle of permanent revolution made possible in the universal history inaugurated by capitalism.'[22] The rejection of society's bad organizations, capitalism and the nuclear family is achieved by this Deleuzean triad by rejecting media exposure and entering into a bonding which defeats both, the nuclear family as well as homosexuality's rigid sexual apartheid. The media seeking to undermine the stability and force of free-form desire is rejected as they achieve their status as the Deleuzean schizos emerging at the end-of-history as the principle of freedom in permanent revolution. As Holland points out, schizophrenia [Deleuze's schizo] is not merely the principle of permanent revolution: it is also the process of revolution itself. It is the *modus operandi* of subject groups, subjugated groups (here, the triad of Mary, Cyst and Muriel), whose very existence and form of operation subvert the dominant mode of organization (in Gems' play it is the nuclear family, gay binary coupling and capitalism, as there is a consensus to reject materialistic public exposure in the media). As Holland puts it, 'the chances for realizing permanent revolution [...] stem from neither individual lines-of-flight nor the operation of subject groups occurring in isolation, but from the intersection and assemblage of individuals and groups into a critical mass whose combined effect it would be to lift the mortgage of the infinite debt and finally liquidate capital and the barriers it poses to freedom and enjoyment.'[23]

Aunt Mary then is a performance of this permanent revolution acted out in a private provincial space occupied by three people who form a beneficient triad which replaces or supplants the Deleuzean Oedipal triad. We have here the Barthesian '*unpredictability* of bliss: the bets are not placed, there can still be a game'. The refusal to play the game (of media exposure and capitalistic exploitation) and the risk of the game of triadic arrangement (a line-of-flight) puts Gems on the pulse of cultural iconology here as her dramaturgy predates the prolific theorizing on gay, bisexual and transgendered bodies in the 1990s.

Franz into April: Freudian Counter-discourse

Franz into April was written for the BBC but was never produced. 'It was felt that the script was too rude for the general public', says Gems in the Foreword. It was, however, produced as a stage play and opened at the ICA as lunchtime theatre in 1977.

Gems' drama with Freud's student and critic, Fritz Perls, as the central character is a study of a coarse and promiscuous man who left behind the legacy of gestalt analysis and a form of therapy which was a counter-discourse to Freud's couch-centred approach.

Gestalt is a broadly interdisciplinary theory which views human beings as open systems in active interaction with their environment. The primacy of the phenomenal is stressed where the world of experience is recognised and seriously addressed as the only immediately given reality and not simply discussed away. The interaction of the individual and the situation in the sense of a dynamic field is said to determine experience and behaviour. As Max Wertheimer explains, 'Once constituted, the Ego is a functional part of the total field.'[24]

In gestalt therapy both the environment and the social context is important: 'The programme to treat the organism as a part in a larger field necessitates the reformulation of the problem as to the relation between organism and environment [...] The total reaction of the organism [has to be considered. The organism] is also one among other men [sic]. When a group of people work together [their Egos become] a meaningfully functioning part of the whole.'[25]

Perls describes himself as 'an early refugee from the Hitler regime'. In 1934 he went to South Africa. It was here, in 1937, that Perls struggled to get out of the quicksand of free associations and fell back on Goldstein's organism-as-a-whole approach. To this he added ecology – 'organism-as-a-whole-embedded-in-environment'. This became 'the Unit' and 'the objective-subjective identity' was born. He refused to do lobotomies in New York and it was only in 1964 that he found a home in the Esalen Institute there. 'What the Bauhaus was in Germany for the creation of a new style in architecture and the arts, Esalen is as a practical centre of the third wave of humanistic psychology'.[26]

Franz into April dramatises a moment when Perls was at Esalen and in his mid-sixties. The play opens with Franz's therapy session: a chair in the centre of the group of analysands functions as the 'hot seat', displacing the one-to-one confessional Freudian couch. ('I work in a group, as in life'. Perls, *Franz into April*, p.35). Gems describes Perls' method as one of 'tough love'. Although 'he was a messy eater, groped girls and was as politically incorrect as you could hope for', Perls was a psychiatrist who 'made sense'.[27] Perls displays the stereotypical attributes of masculinity: he is 'hard, aggressive, strong, dominant, remote, powerful [...] rational [...] competitive' and above all, sexist.[28]

The scene is meta-dramatic, commenting on stage and performance as the members of the therapy group sit within the bounds of the audience. Since the stage extends into the audience, Franz's cutting comments to his analysands are addressed to the audience: 'you are bored – upset? ... not getting your money's worth'. One of the analysands rises from the audience and makes her way along the row of chairs on stage (*Franz into April*, p.5). As he goads Paula, he turns to the audience-turned-analysands and comments caustically: 'All alone! Look at her, ladies and gentlemen ... what a pitiful sight ... so sad ... so sad ...' (p. 12).

The Fritz Perls (Franz) of the play is a man of large appetites, both sensual and sexual. Perhaps, as the young nurse, April, puts it, he's 'just a dirty old man' (p. 23). Whatever Perls is like in person he is a large figure both, in the play and in the world of psychoanalysis and gestalt therapy. This is Freud's disciple who broke away, questioning dogma even before the notion of the Ego had become dogmatic practice as he strove to take into account the social context. He saw the couch as repressive:

> Why the couch, this ikon of psychoanalysis? Freud couldn't bear to look anyone in the face, he was too phobic! So ... as a result ... I cease to worship. I give up my guru. (p. 29)

Perls prefigures Michel Foucault's critique of the confessional and what Foucault describes as 'Freud's conformism [and] the normalizing functions of psychoanalysis'[29] which is a symptom of the increasing scope of the confessional in western societies.[30]

Freud's couch was but another version – a medical one – of the centuries-old confessional which 'attributed more and more importance [...] to all the insinuations of the flesh: thoughts, desires, voluptuous imaginings, delectations, combined movements of the body and soul.'[31] It is this transformation of the Christian pastoral into medical discourse[32] that Perls seems to find objectionable. His open and unabashed sexuality is the counter-discourse to Freudian repression, the latter a symptom of the spread of the repressive confessional into western discourse.

> when I start to confess that what I really enjoy is to look at a woman's genitals, suddenly there is the scrape of his chair and he is sitting closer, closer. Every week I must think up better stories, he can't get enough of it! ... in the end he is waiting mit the schnapps to help loosen me up – you are a Don Juan, he says, and when he sees me in the street he lifts his hat! Ach, what we do to please! – you know that the patients of Freud had Freudian dreams, those of Jung had Jungian dreams. (p. 35)

Perls is tough, almost to the point of cruelty it seems, although this quality seems to elicit the appropriate response from the analysand. In the session in act II he dives straight into the heart of the problem with no qualms as Wayne sits in the hot seat: 'Tell us about your mother', and, brutally: 'she's dead [...] Those ashes ... they are not your mother [...] she's probably in there with a coupla bums and a garment salesman, who knows?'(p.61). The session ends painfully yet successfully as Wayne breaks down, cries and splutters, 'She was a lousy mother. I didn't love her'. Franz is able to get Wayne to admit that he was competing with his mother, the star, and the attachment to her ashes, which Wayne carries everywhere, is symptomatic of his refusal to admit she was an inadequate mother. Perls' 'extreme masculinity'[33] – almost machismo – offsets Wayne's apparent fragility. In a perverse way, Perls' harshness seems more honest than the new soft masculinity. Kenneth MacKinnon speaks of the new masculinity which is softer and more feminized 'without addressing patriarchal power or capitalist work relations. This softening of masculinity may have little to do with female emancipation or empowerment. The most cynical interpretation would be that, in order for masculinity to remain hegemonic, it must admit the feminine at certain historical moments.'[34] Admittedly, the dominant discourse of masculinity is always in a process of renewal – it constantly shifts its parameters and boundaries, restructuring itself to maintain the hierarchy of gender. Within this hierarchy, the dominant is so because of its controlling power, and Perls fulfils this role as analyst. Perhaps he is so successful at his version of therapy (tough love) because he occupies unquestioningly the position of command, which is, admittedly hegemonic, as the role is accepted, participated in

– and perhaps needed – by his clients. His role 'serves as an example of the core of his message: to learn to grow up and become self-responsible. His command role [provides] a model by which his patients may overcome their own oppression.'[35]

Through the play we see an incisive rethinking of and debunking of Freud. As Franz puts it, '[Freud] thought a person would not mature because of a childhood trauma – it is the other way around!' (p. 81) Franz hypothesizes that childhood is a 'prison of invented memory' which justifies the individual's 'unwillingness to grow up.' He believes individuals 'project some part of [their] potential' into others, thereby seeking their approval to validate and, indeed, construct their sense of self. And 'this potential turns against us' as we exist and 'see ourselves as an imagined sum of the judgements of others'. (p. 64). Self-discovery, for Franz, is a rejection of demands from without and a 'turning towards the light' in a celebration of a re-constructed self. (pp. 64–5). His hypothesis was that we have to break free from the shape we were forced into as children by controlling adults and find ourselves by taking charge and recreating our own lives. He recommends that we create circumstances and make them happen: 'only by making appropriate demand can we be truly unselfish' (p. 83). Insistent that we make our own lives by rejecting childhood constructions, Fritz Perls' is a severe critique of Freud's insistence that the traumas of childhood have a determining influence on our adult lives. Perls' methods offer a way forward, out of the prisons of our pasts, thus prefiguring the Foucauldian injunction: 'not to discover what we are, but to refuse what we are', thus promoting 'new forms of subjectivity through refusal'.[36]

STANLEY: MASCULINITY IN CRISIS

Farewell (sweet *Cooke-ham*) where I first obtain'd
Grace from that Grace where perfit Grace remain'd,
And where the Muses gave their full consent,
I should have power the virtuous to content:
Where princely Palace will'd me to indite,
The sacred Storie of the Soules delight. [ll. 1–6]

[…]

In these sweet woods how often did you walke,
With Christ and his Apostles there to talke;
Placing his holy writ in some faire tree,
To meditate what you therein did see:

With *Moyses* you did mount his holy Hill,
To know his pleasure, and performe his Will. [ll. 81–86]
(Aemilia Lanyer, 'The Description of Cooke-ham')[37]

Stanley Spencer is one of the most highly regarded of all English artists. Famous for immortalizing the Berkshire village of Cookham where he was born and spent much of his life, influenced by the art of Giotto di Bondone (1267–1337), who painted traditional religious subjects in pre-Renaissance Italy, Stanley Spencer is best known for paintings of Biblical subjects set in and around Cookham, in particular, *The Resurrection, Cookham*. He may also have read and been influenced by Aemilia Lanyer's poem which 'describes' Cookham in much the same religious and visionary fashion as later concretized in Spencer's art.[38] He revelled in the intense ordinariness of the world he inhabited, and his mature art fuses oppositions to create a spiritual unity: religion and sex mingle, as do the real and the imaginary, public and private, the young and the old, the self and other. His art grew out of places, experiences and social relations which enriched his imagination. His mystical and visionary qualities were grounded in the material: in the landscapes, homes and human relationships which he felt so strongly.[39]

Spencer's life and art was a celebration of sex, and his unconventional understanding of relationships led to his fixation on Patricia Preece, a Slade-trained painter like himself. He divorced Hilda Carline, also an artist,[40] to marry Preece. He signed over his house to Preece, who brought her lifelong lesbian lover, Dorothy Hepworth, with her and refused to consummate the marriage. After gaining possession of Spencer's money and property, Preece threw him out. Spencer attempted a reconciliation with Hilda, who refused him. He loved Hilda Carline to the end of his days, and in the year of his own death (1959) he was still writing her love letters although she was long dead.[41]

For the working-class boy, Preece seemed to embody the wealth of the substantial houses in mock-Tudor style in Cookham which 'had always seemed to him as supernatural beings [...] He used to peer in through gates and hedges, trying to catch a glimpse of elegance and luxury: for he never set foot in any such place, unless it was to deliver something at the kitchen door.'[42]

He was thirty-two and still a virgin when he became Hilda's lover in 1923. He began painting the *Resurrection* that year.[43] It was not overtly sexual, but the awakening to a new vision of paradise on earth, a symbolic resurrection, would be a most natural feeling in one suddenly exploring the long delayed pleasures of manhood.[44]

In the book Louise Collis ghostwrote for Patricia Preece, she describes the planned painting of the Tower of Babel and Stanley's unique personality: 'It would be quite natural, according to his system of ideas, to put Hilda, his children, Elsie [his maid], his father, himself and me into the Tower of Babel. I have since thought that if he had carried his scheme through it would have perfectly symbolized his life and character. For really he spoke a different language from other human beings. The meanings he attached to ordinary words and deeds were quite his own, born of a unique confusion of ideas. The incoherence of much of his conversation and the extraordinary domestic arrangements he tried to make on our marriage in 1937 seem in retrospect more suited to the architect of a Tower of Babel than anything.'[45]

Like Spencer's paintings which often show a divide between the spiritual and the material which conjoin to produce one unified work of art, Gems' play separates the stage space between Preece and Carline. Act I, scene ix in particular has Hilda, his spiritual love, in a state of breakdown as Stanley fastens an expensive necklace around Patricia's neck. In this scene Patricia symbolises Stanley's fantasy personified and materialized. Patricia also fantasizes: for her it is the jewels and money which she can get from Stanley. Both represent the object-of-desire in the eyes of the other: both are material fantasies expressed very differently. Stanley lavished money and jewels on Patricia, whilst paying very little attention to Hilda and the children's well-being. We see a divide in the stage space between the material (Preece) and the spiritual (Carline), one in darkness, the other in light:

> He opens a ring box. PATRICIA takes out the engagement ring, puts it on her finger, displays it to DOROTHY, who shrugs and turns away. HILDA, bereft, sits small in her chair. PATRICIA changes for the wedding. DOROTHY tries on a hat. PATRICIA shakes her head. STANLEY puts on a clean shirt, suit and tie.

> Hilda: [...] How can you be happy when you know I'm in such a plight? What you're doing is murder. (I, ix)

Stanley was selfish in his relationships with women. He typically wanted more than one:

> What I want to know is, why must a man have only one woman? [... Polygamy is] a sign of intelligence. I can reach the most intense state of being and awareness, and in each case it is utterly sincere. I feel total fusion and ecstasy with Hilda ... and with Patricia. [...] I need a dozen homes – that's what I'd like, with me as father in each. (II, iv)

It's the way all men want it if they'd only be honest and speak up. I'd like twenty wives … I want to be able to go from one house to another … be made welcome … I'd like to – when one of them isn't, or when … or having children … (II, vi)

His obsession with Preece led to several nudes which are stark and honest to the point where every blue vein is visible, every crease exposed. These hyper-realist nudes of Patricia Preece anticipate by some decades the grotesque nudes which have made Lucian Freud famous.[46]

The whole of my life in art has been a slow realisation of the mystery of sex! It is the key to everything! […] Hilda, I am convinced that the erotic is the essence of religion. I intend to spend the rest of my life reaching the spiritual through the physical … that personal experience you get when you draw someone's body – isn't that the most wonderful sexual experience? (II, v)

His attitude of open and unashamed sexuality was novel in a climate he saw as repressed:

I know you middle classes are all the same, separate bedrooms, ooh, don't come too close, never look you in the eye, you must all be experts on foreheads, it's what you look at when you talk. Well, I'm not like that, and I won't be, and I don't desire to be. (II, vi)

Yet, despite Stanley's ideal of attaining a union with several other women, he never found a spiritual quality in any of his encounters. Ironically it was Hilda who represented the spiritual ecstasy and union which he so sought in life and his art:

you're such a marvellous present to me, and I'm so grateful … I want to paint an altar-piece of you […] you're so deep! (II, ix)

Patricia was his material triumph, a 'social vanity'. In Gems' play he admits he had 'no spiritual relationship with her […] eyes colder than a mortuary slab'. (II, x) His relationship with Hilda betrayed what Roger Horrocks calls 'a crisis of masculinity'.[47] With Hilda he could be most himself – the war veteran could cry and be a child. The idealised Patricia, whom he worships from afar, is the material divide from his wife with whom he achieves intimacy. It could be possible that as a modern male and artist Stanley was suffocated by the intimacy he achieved with Hilda thereby desiring a more dispassionate and idealised relationship. T. S. Eliot, Horrocks reminds us, wrote of the difference between the modern artist (poet) and the (so-called) Metaphysical poets: thought and feeling have been separate since the seventeenth century when 'a dissociation of sensibility set in, from which we have never recovered.' Horrocks links Eliot's claim with that of D. H. Lawrence who sees man's 'loss of passion' as central to the masculine crisis since the eighteenth century. The Renaissance bred ideas of male reason and objectivity and scientific thought which caused a fundamental crisis in the male as they began to separate thought from feeling. In Stanley both thought and feeling reside – he is able to express both sides of his dichotomized personality but with two very different women. However, Patricia, by the social codes of the early part of the twentieth century represents the masculine in her actively independent lifestyle and liaison with a woman. Her coldness, reason and objectivity thrust her into a masculine space which inevitably contrasts with Stanley's stereotypically feminine mode of feeling and passion. Thus, it is Patricia who possesses the power of a conventionally masculine domain which exposes Stanley's male crisis. Patricia's masculinity, which is an effect of her autonomy in her particular time period as well as her attachment to a woman, exposes a kind of effeminacy in Stanley, which is exacerbated by the rejection by Hilda. That he was still writing to Hilda after her death reveals a dependency and attachment which are regressive.

The divide in his life, between the banal and material ordinariness of life and the spiritual ecstasy he craved for, found expression in and gave life to his art. Gems' play, directed by John Caird for the National Theatre, creatively merges stage space to express this division of self which is expressed as an artistic unity. Stanley Spencer's intense emotional attachment and regressive dependency, expressed itself in the act of writing Hilda love letters even till the year of his death in 1959. Hilda Carline died in 1950. His intense spirituality enabled him to believe he had a close communion with his first wife after she died. The play ends on an epiphany as he communes with nature and the dead Hilda whilst he paints: 'this is for your altar-piece. [...] It makes me feel closer to Heaven with you there.' His belief that heaven could be reached by means of translating the ordinary into art, as well as his tendency to put himself into paintings, echoes Michelangelo's egoistic vision as the play ends: 'an artist is the mediator between God and man.' (II, xiv)

GARIBALDI: MASCULINITY AS MYTH

Garibaldi, Si! is a play which explores what Pam Gems calls 'an international star'.[48] The formation of the nation-state is represented here as something to be celebrated. The freedom from foreign domination and a celebration of the oneness of peoples and democracy are ideals Garibaldi and the makers of the Italian nation-state aspire to. A united and democratic Italy formulates itself under the direction of the fearless

Giuseppe Garibaldi (1807–1882) who is a modern hero. Unification means freedom from imperialism and foreign intervention from Austria and France as well as the demise of the papal states. Garibaldi was the foremost military figure and popular hero of the age of Italian unification known as the Risorgimento. With Cavour and Mazzini he is deemed one of the makers of Modern Italy. Cavour is considered the "brain of unification," Mazzini the "sou," and Garibaldi the "sword." For his battles on behalf of freedom in Latin America, Italy, and later France, he has been dubbed the "Hero of Two Worlds." Born in Nice, when the city was controlled by France, to Domenico Garibaldi and Rosa Raimondi, his family was involved in the coastal trade. A sailor in the Mediterranean Sea, he was certified a merchant captain in 1832. During a journey to Taganrog in the Black Sea, he was initiated into the Italian national movement by a fellow Ligurian, Giovanni Battista Cuneo. In 1833 he ventured to Marseilles where he met Mazzini and enrolled in his *Giovane Italia* or Young Italy. Mazzini had a profound impact on Garibaldi, who would always acknowledge this patriot as "the master."[49]

In February 1834 he participated in an abortive Mazzinian insurrection in Piedmont, was sentenced to death in absentia by a Genoese court, and fled to Marseilles. The exile sailed first to Tunisia eventually finding his way to Brazil, where he encountered Anna Maria Ribeiro da Silva, "Anita," a woman of Portuguese and Indian descent, who became his lover, companion in arms, and wife. With other Italian exiles and republicans he fought on behalf of the separatists of the Rio Grande do Sul and the Uruguayans who opposed the Argentinean dictator Jan Manuel do Rosas. Calling on the Italians of Montevideo, Garibaldi formed the Italian Legion in 1843, whose black flag represented Italy in mourning while the volcano at its center symbolized the dormant power in their homeland. It was in Uruguay that the legion first sported the red shirts, obtained from a factory in Montevideo which had intended to export them to the slaughter houses of Argentina. It was to become the symbol of Garibaldi and his followers. The formation of his force of volunteers, his mastery of the techniques of guerilla warfare, his opposition to Brazilian and Argentinean imperialism, and his victories in the battles of Cerro and Sant'Antonio in 1846 not only assured the freedom of Uruguay but made him and his followers heroes in Italy and Europe. The fate of his patria continued to preoccupy Garibaldi.[49]

The election of Giovanni Mastai-Ferretti as Pope Pius IX in 1846 led many to believe he was the liberal pope prophesied by Gioberti, who would provide the leadership for the unification of Italy. From his exile Mazzini applauded the first reforms of Pio Nono. In 1847 Garibaldi offered the apostolic nuncio at Rio de Janeiro Bedini, the service of his Italian Legion for the liberation of the peninsula. News of the outbreak of revolution in Palermo in January 1848, and revolutionary agitation elsewhere in Italy, encouraged Garibaldi to lead some sixty members of his legion home. He offered his services to Charles Albert and the Piedmontese who initiated the first war for the liberation of Italy, but found his effort spurned. Rebuffed by the Piedmonese, he and his followers crossed into Lombardy where they offered assistance to the provisional government of Milan.[49] The play begins and ends in his retirement and need for peace over power.

Giuseppe Garibaldi is the ideal of the western military icon, one who does not kill for pleasure but expediently in defence and to unify the country. For him the means (killing) must be justified by the ends. In a strange parallel with Queen Christina, Garibaldi, a very masculine icon is one whose construction allows femininity to seep through in a margin of excess; a liminal space he cannot help but inhabit even in the display of his masculinity. This libidinal excess manifests itself in Garibaldi's frequent exhortations to the Garibaldini not to kill – this is what makes him a modern myth.

> Garibaldi: A soldier exists to honour life. He is there for the protection of his wife – his children – his village, his town, his country – and – therefore – *not one life is to be wasted!*

> Garibaldini are fighters – not killers. [...] kill only in the defence of the life of your friend. [...] When you kill you kill an Italian – you kill your brother. (Scene viii, p.27)

The meeting with the English news researcher Campion carries the play forward and unites the scenes as his memories of meeting Garibaldi take us from Sicily to Naples to Rome which Garibaldi frees and unites as modern Italy takes shape. The interview by a foreign news researcher brings Garibaldi into focus as a myth and an icon as does his meeting with Alfred, Lord Tennyson which symbolises the reception he received in England. The masculinity myth is perpetrated through this play as Garibaldi demonstrates the stereotypical masculine traits of toughness, stoicism and courage in the face of adversity. Yet, the play demonstrates the changing nature of masculinity, not as crisis, but as a positive space for men. Garibaldi, in spite of being a military hero, is portrayed almost as a new man; not the superficial softening and feminization of masculinity cynically exposed by Kenneth MacKinnon as a space which increasingly does not address the relations of patriarchal and capitalist power, admitting femininity to maintain the hegemonic sway of gender; but a liminal space of gendering which is as Eve Kosofsky Sedgwick describes it, 'orthogonal'; a perpendicular relation which allows both men and women to occupy the spaces of masculine and feminine.[50] *Garibaldi* is one of Gems' plays about a masculine conqueror which throws into juxtaposition the very many plays about women myth-makers. A play about courage and determination, *Garibaldi, Si!* is about an icon who is 'anti-religious and anti-royal': 'an audacious, resourceful man, capable of idiocy, a man of heart, a mixture of Ulysses and Hercules'.[51] This play celebrates the space of masculine military determination mixed with the liminal space of the feminine ideals of the need for family and peace.

NOTES

1. H. Benjamin, *The Transsexual Phenomenon*, Julian Press, 1966, p.37.

2. Letter to the author from Jonathan Gems, 18 April 2004.

3. Alan Sinfield, 'Transgender and les/bi/gay identities' in David Alderson and Linda Anderson (eds.), *Territories of Desire in Queer Culture: Reconfiguring contemporary boundaries*, Manchester University Press, 2000, p.150. The particular constraint that so-called identity positions place on the individual as subject, deny a complete agency of the subject-individual in society. Identity classifications reduce individuals to state functions or functions of the aspects of social, political, ethical boundaries that separate us from ourselves.

4. Alan Sinfield paraphrasing Jay Prosser. Alan Sinfield, 'Transgender and les/bi/gay identities' in David Alderson and Linda Anderson (eds.), *Territories of Desire in Queer Culture: Reconfiguring contemporary boundaries*, Manchester University Press, 2000, p.163 n.1. Jay Prosser, 'Transgender' in Andy Medhurst and Sally R. Munt (eds.), *Lesbian and Gay Studies: A Critical Introduction*, Cassell, 1997.

5. See 'Shinjuku Boys' in Alan Sinfield, 'Transgender and les/bi/gay identities' in David Alderson and Linda Anderson (eds.), *Territories of Desire in Queer Culture: Reconfiguring contemporary boundaries*, Manchester University Press, 2000, pp.150–152.

6. Thus defined in the 'Diagnostic and Statistical Manual of Mental Disorders' of the American Psychiatric Association as late as 1987. See Richard F. Docter, *Transvestites and Transsexuals: Toward a Theory of Cross-Gender Behaviour*, Plenium Press, 1988, p. viii and chapter 2.

7. Richard F. Docter, *Transvestites and Transsexuals: Toward a Theory of Cross-Gender Behaviour*, Plenium Press, 1988, p. vii.

8. Richard F. Docter, *Transvestites and Transsexuals: Toward a Theory of Cross-Gender Behaviour*, Plenium Press, 1988, pp.1–3.

9. Richard F. Docter, *Transvestites and Transsexuals: Toward a Theory of Cross-Gender Behaviour*, Plenium Press, 1988, p.6

10. Tennessee Williams, *Penguin Plays: Sweet Bird of Youth / A Streetcar Named Desire / The Glass Menagerie*, Penguin Books, 1959.

11. Laurence Senelick, *The Changing Room: Sex, Drag and Theatre*, Routledge, 2000, pp. 298ff.

12. Richard Howard, 'A Note on the Text', in Roland Barthes, *The Pleasure of the Text* [*Le Plaisir du texte*, 1973] trans. Richard Miller, Farrar, Straus and Giroux, 1975, pp. v–vi.

13. Kenneth Marlowe, *The Male Homosexual*, Los Angeles: Medco, 1968, pp. 12–13. Quoted in Alan Sinfield, 'Transgender and les/bi/gay identities', p.157.

14. Quentin Crisp, *The Naked Civil Servant*, Plume, 1977, p.21. Quoted in Alan Sinfield, 'Transgender and les/bi/gay identities', p.157.

15. Alan Sinfield, 'Transgender and les/bi/gay identities', p.157.

16. Lesley Ferris, ed., *Crossing the Stage: Controversies on Cross Dressing*, Routledge, 1993, pp. 4–5.

17. Michel Foucault, Introduction to *Herculine Barbin: Being the Recently Discovered Memoirs of a Nineteenth-Century French Hermaphrodite*, *[Herculine Barbin, dite Alexina B.]*, pub. Gallimard, 1978, trans. Richard McDougall, The Harvester Press, 1980, p.vii.

18. Judith Butler, *Gender Trouble: Feminism and the Subversion of Identity*, Routledge, 1990, p.97.

19. Susan Carlson, 'Revisionary Endings: Pam Gems *Aunt Mary* and *Camille*', in Lynda Hart, ed., *Making a Spectacle: Feminist Essays on Contemporary Theatre*, University of Michigan Press, 1989, p.103.

20. See Judith Butler, 'Variations on Sex and Gender', in Seyla Benhabib and Drucilla Cornell, eds., *Feminism As Critique*, Oxford University Press, 1987.

21. Judith Butler, *Bodies that Matter*, pp.285–286.

22. Eugene W. Holland, *Deleuze and Guattari's Anti-Oedipus: Introduction to Schizoanalysis*, Routledge, 1999. p.121.

23. Eugene W. Holland, *Deleuze and Guattari's Anti-Oedipus: Introduction to Schizoanalysis*, Routledge, 1999, p. 123.

24. Max Wertheimer, lecture on gestalt theory, 1924, http://www.enabling.org/ia/gestalt/gerhards/wert1.html. Also read 'Capitalism and Schizophrenia: *The Skriker* as Oedipus and Anti-Oedipus' in *Breaking the Bounds: British Feminist Dramatists Writing in the Mainstream since c. 1980*, American University Studies: Series XXVI, Vol.31, Peter Lang, 2003, p.77ff.

25. http://www.enabling.org/ia/gestalt/gerhards/wert1.html.

26. Fritz Perls, *Ego, Hunger and Aggression*, Random House, 1969.

27. Pam Gems, Foreword, *Franz into April*.

28. See John MacInnes, *The End of Masculinity*, Open University Press, 1998, p. 14.

29. Michel Foucault, *The History of Sexuality*, Vol. I, Penguin, 1990, p.5

30. Michel Foucault, *The History of Sexuality*, Vol. I, Penguin, 1990, p.19

31. Michel Foucault, *The History of Sexuality*, Vol. I, Penguin, 1990, p. 19

32. Michel Foucault, *The History of Sexuality*, Vol. I, Penguin, 1990, see p.21

33. See Roger Horrocks, *Masculinity in Crisis*, Macmillan, 1994, p.89.

34. Kenneth MacKinnon, *Representing Men*, Arnold, 1993, p.15.

35. Jonathan Gems in a letter to the author, 18 April 2004.

36. See Michel Foucault's *Afterword*, 'The Subject and Power', to Hubert Dreyfus and Paul Rabinow, *Michel Foucault: Beyond Structuralism and Hermeneutics*, University of Chicago Press, 1982, p.208.

37. In *The Penguin Book of Renaissance Verse 1509–1659*, ed. David Norbrook, Penguin, 1992. p. 414.

38. Lanyer evokes the mythical Phoenix, Phoebus and Philomela besides the Biblical figures of Moses, David, Joseph and Christ, all of who lend Dorset and 'Cookeham' their mysterious and mytho-religious quality which is also found in Spencer.

39. Kitty Hauser, *Stanley Spencer*, Princeton University Press, 2001.

40. See Timothy Wilcox, ed., *The Art of Hilda Carline, Mrs. Stanley Spencer*, Lincolnshire County Council, the Usher Gallery, 1999.

41. Kitty Hauser, *Stanley Spencer*, Princeton University Press, 2001; Robert Fulford, *The National Post*, 23 October 2001. For Preece's point of view, see her ghostwritten book, Louise Collis, *A Private View of Stanley Spencer*, William Heinemann Ltd, 1972.

42. Louise Collis, *A Private View of Stanley Spencer*, William Heinemann Ltd, 1972, p.32.

43. See especially Kenneth Pople's biography, *Stanley Spencer*, William Collins, 1991, p. 224ff.

44. Louise Collis, *A Private View of Stanley Spencer*, William Heinemann Ltd, 1972, p.30.

45. Louise Collis, *A Private View of Stanley Spencer*, William Heinemann Ltd, 1972, p.52-3.

46. Robert Fulford, *The National Post*, 23 October 2001.

47. Roger Horrocks, *Masculinity in Crisis*, Macmillan, 1994, p.7.

48. In the *Foreword* to *Garibaldi, Si!*

49. Compiled by James Chastain. http://www.ohiou.edu/~chastain/dh/gari.htm.Cecchini, Ezio. "Le Campagne di Garibaldi. 1849." *Rivista Militare* 105 (1982, n.2), 197-205; Coppa, Frank J. *The Origins of the Italian Wars of Independence*. London and New York: Longman, 1992; Garibaldi, Giuseppe. *Autobiography*, trans. A Werner. New York: Howard Fertig, 1971; Garibaldi, Giuseppe. *Memoire*, ed. Ugoberto Alfessio Grimaldi. Verona: Bertani editore, 1972; Ridley, Joseph. *Garibaldi*. New York: Viking, 1976; Trevelyan, George Macaulay. *Garibaldi and the Thousand*. New York: Longman, 1948; Ugolini, Romano. *Garibaldi. Genesi di un mito*. Rome: Ateneo, 1982.

50. Roger Horrocks, *Masculinity in Crisis*, Macmillan, 1994, p.62; Roger Horrocks, *Male Myths and Icons: Masculininity in Popular Culture*, Macmillan, 1995; Kenneth MacKinnon, *Representing Men*, Arnold, 2003, p.15; Eve Kosofsky Sedgwick, 'Gosh, Boy George, you must be awfully secure in your masculinity!', in Maurice Berger, Brian Wallis and Simon Watson (eds.) *Constructing Masculinity*, Routledge, 1995, pp.15–16.

51. *Foreword*, by Pam Gems.

4

NEGOTIATING A SPACE FOR 'THE OTHER'

[We] need the Other in order to realize fully all the structures of [our] being.[1]

Not content to portray the variations in the queer spaces of gender, relationships and identity formation, Gems also writes the cultural Other. The perspective of these plays shifts to incorporate a racial and cultural inclusion, bringing into focus the construction of English identities as they are juxtaposed with their Others in all their queernesses.

EBBA: BEING AND NON-BEING

Ebba, a play not yet on the stage at the time of writing, can be seen as a study in comparative culture where the difference of the other (dispossessed Russia) defines what it means to be middle class and English today whilst they both need and depend mutually on each other to realize fully their identities and all the structures of their being. The beautiful Russian's presence in England throws the particular Englishness of the other players of the drama into relief. Ebba exists – is – as the English others see her. She is revealed to us as their Russian other by the very nature of their perception of her otherness. As Sartre would have it, the English others are *of themselves* only *before her other*, that is, their identity occupies a relative position in order to fully come into being. The structures of both sets of others 'are inseparable. But at the same time I need the other in order to realise fully all the structures of my being.' The existence of the other and the relation of one's being to that of the other are important.[2]

Ebba is projected as being an Other by her Russianness; however it is her amorality which sets her apart to seemingly shock and make apparent the English middle-class reserve she finds herself amidst. An amorality in terms of frequent sexual encounters, using rich men to pay for her, stealing from shops is of course not particularly Russian at all; it is merely the sensibilities of those around her that are shocked; but it equally constructs a (fictitious) sense of Englishness as Other to these qualities. Her forthrightness about her amorality is particularly refreshing, but Ebba is merely a European Other, similar or perhaps the same, which is of course what Sartre meant. In Sartrean terms the 'other' is merely another being who is separate from the self – different and the same – and it is perhaps in this definition that the Russianness of her other and the Englishness of the other players that is contrasted as well as constructed. After Sartre, postcolonial studies took the notion of the 'Other' as distinguished from the 'other' from Jacques Lacan and applied it to postcolonial thought about the colonial and colonized subject much like the Hegelian dialectical construct of Master and Slave. The notion of the Other in terms of the subject in relation to the imperial central power is explored in two of Gems' earlier plays. The mastered subject – the Other – is not, in Gems, necessarily the stereotypical dependant-colonized of postcolonial theories. S/he is not necessarily excised or edited as Edward Said would have us believe, but instead, exists in a complex relationship with the colonizer or the foreign central power. Literary and dramatic work such as this puts notions of colonizer-colonized, master-slave, imperial subject-imperial power into a more sophisticated interface and reveals the dichotomized theorizing of postcolonial studies as somewhat uncritical and non-problematized. Gems' plays date from the 1970s onwards and contest what often seem the myths of postcolonial theory onwards from Edward Said's work on what was termed Orientalism.

Pam Gems' delineation of the native other is found in her early play, *Go West, Young Woman* which is located in colonial America and in *Deborah's Daughter* which is set in Northern Africa. Here Gems reinterprets East-West relations, rescuing them from the stereotype laid out in traditional discourse or even seemingly radical books like Said's *Orientalism*. Her mythologies occupy the queer spaces of racial discourse.

GO WEST, YOUNG WOMAN AND DEBORAH'S DAUGHTER: A DISCOURSE OF GENDER, POWER AND THE OTHER

Orientalism, Edward Said's early influential text which opened up the discipline of postcolonial theorizing across the globe since its publication in 1978 proves useful in the generalized juxtaposing of not merely East and West as he does, but in analysing any contradictory and oppositional hierarchical relationship between racialized

Others and a dominant class. Here, I analyse the departures that Gems' second full-length play (after *Betty's Wonderful Christmas*), and her first overtly feminist play makes from Said's now largely outdated text. Written for the Women's Theatre Group, *Go West, Young Woman* was their first production at the Roundhouse Theatre in Camden in 1974. The script is a narrative which ostensibly celebrates the making of America but subversively problematizes what appears to be the simplistic hierarchical relationship between the native Indian whose territory it originally is, and the colonial presence of the white settlers in what is to them a newfound land. It throws up a series of contradictions which creatively destabilize not merely colonial discourse but also Said's contention that white European authors write of the Other in monolithic and non-contradictory terms by means of editing and excision. In this piece, the settlers themselves are placed in hierarchical relationships, both economic and gender-based, complicating their responses to the native Indians who themselves are by no means necessarily portrayed as the racial savage of the stereotypical white texts spoken of by Said in the 1970s. Gems' literary and theatrical exercise acknowledges the role and agency of the other in this piece written as early as 1974 when race, its subject's agency, the complex hierarchizations which accompany the subjectivities of both the colonizer and the colonized were barely regarded as fashionable for the white English dramatist.

Go West is also about the pioneer women who founded modern feminism. It subverts one of the founding myths of the United States, the oft-repeated story of settlers heading west across America, fighting hardships and Indians. The title of the play is also an inversion of Horace Greeley's famous advice to the young abolitionist Josiah B. Grinnell: "Go West, young man, go West." While this origin myth has always been a celebration of male courage and fortitude, here the women are the protagonists in the typical gendered writing of Pam Gems. The play traverses the spaces of colonial America, as the settlers invade to make a life in the newly opened Territories. Scene ii opens with incipient travellers to the west. Land is the primary reason for giving up old acquaintances and neighbours to journey into the heart of the west. The territorial imperative drove Europe to colonize three quarters of the globe since the world was 'discovered'.[3]

Rich and poor make their way to California. Whilst scene v has two young women fitted with tailor-made riding habits to ride out into the west, scene iv has a young couple, with the woman heavily pregnant, make their way across America with a handcart and a few provisions. Poor immigrants who serve as laundresses and maids are among the great exodus to the west. Scene iii gives us Asa Mercer, more famous for bringing shiploads of women around Cape Horn to the then-wild Puget Sound area in the 1860s than for first presiding over one of the great research universities of the United States. In 1864, he visited the East Coast and enlisted a group of "New England school marms" to journey west on the *Torrent*. The members of that party married quickly, so Mercer repeated his mission. In 1866, he signed up 200 women to take the steamer *Continental*. "No more curious or suggestive exodus ever took place," said *Harper's Weekly*. The voyage lasted 3½ months. Many of those women married quickly as well. According to several accounts, the Puget Sound today is said to be populated with descendants of the "Mercer Girls."[4]

We also see Catherine Beecher, famous for being an educator in America in the 1800s.[5] Only described as 'a soberly dressed woman', she calls the young women out to the west: Wives are needed, and teachers and nurses. The purpose is 'noble': 'A whole generation of children is in danger of being deprived of mental and moral instruction [...] Go west where our children are crying out for your devotion and your example. I implore you to answer the challenge – go west, young woman!' (I, iii, pp.5–6)

Even though *Go West, Young Woman* purports to be 'about the role of women in America in the nineteenth century. In the east – and in the west'[6] the play opens with the soliloquy of the native. After all, 'the wild west' was 'Indian' country. American history begins with the decimation of the so-called American Indians. Thus, Gems makes American Indians central to her piece about colonial America. The native's opening cry is a celebration of the rich land, the 'Crow Country' which rightfully belongs to him: 'The air is sweet, the grasses are fresh, and bright streams flow out of the snowbanks.' It sings of plenitude: 'You give us the elk, the deer, the antelope, and our buffalo are fine and large. You give us cottonwood bark for our horses, and the cool air of high places.' Yet, the native's cry will not be heard: 'Preserve us, oh great Grandfather, from all enemies.'

Gems creates a space for the unspoken in colonial American discourse, the native American Indian. Although this space cannot be classified as the Orient, some analogies from Edward Said's work *Orientalism* are pertinent here. Just as Europe created an Orient in a nexus of knowledge and power which in creating the Orient obliterated the Oriental as human being,[7] so the European settlers similarly obliterated the native Indian. Gems gives the Amer-Indian subaltern a voice thereby re-presenting him and implicating him in the process of writing a play in a manner seldom seen amongst Said's European writers of fiction. That the subaltern cannot be spoken for without re-presentation is Said's concurrence; however, Gems' attempt to create the space of American colonization cannot but take into account the decimation of the native.

Exploring with a dexterity the racial prejudice and hatred in the heart of colonial America, Gems does not exclude, displace or make supererogatory the space of the subaltern native; she does not edit.[8] In a manner befitting the Occidental, the young women of Gems play fantasize about and fetishize the Indian.

Lizzie and Annie, giggling over a book.

Lizzie (reading) 'They were the best looking Indians I ever saw [...] The glare of the fire fell on their bare, brawny arms and naked bodies' ... naked bodies! (they giggle) (I, v, p.7)

Gems takes the rough and arduous journey of the European traveller crossing America for gold and land and displays the European reduced to an unhygienic destitute creature who will stop at nothing till he acquires possessions he has only dreamed of. In the midst of this frenzied quest for territory and gold, the young women fetishize and fantasize about the subaltern presence who remains not at the threshold or absent as in much colonial writing but looms large in this piece. She does not edit, she does not excise in the manner of Said's Edward William Lane – she details the attraction-repulsion the European typically faces when looking at his other. In this scene we also see the process of 'othering' taking place as the European women define and delineate the Amer-Indian as different (savage) to the (civilized) white man, excluding and undermining the Amer-Indian as the white man is seen as hygienic and clean making him a marker of moral power in the discourse of conquest and rule of the native's territory:

Annie (Looking at the Indian) He looks quite human – apart from being swart in the face.

Emma: Don't get too close, girls.
          [...]
Lizzie: Imagine wearing a blanket in this heat!
Emma: I wonder how he came by that, that's a white man's blanket. Don't get too close, I warrant he's full of bugs. (I, viii, p.13)

Gems' play becomes far richer and more complex when she attempts to detail the attraction felt by the Amer-Indian for the European other. The Amer-Indian is as fascinated by the white wo/man as s/he is with the Amer-Indian.

an Indian has walked in through the door. He is partially naked, and painted. Annie stands, her mouth open. [...] [Lizzie] sees the Indian and screams. The Indian advances on Annie and inspects her. He is fascinated by her yellow hair. [...] He takes out his knife. Lizzie trembles violently. He lifts a lock of Annie's hair. Once she realises that he does not intend to scalp her, she rallies. She picks up a pair of scissors and cuts a piece of her hair for him. He slices off a lock of his hair with his knife and gives it to her, and goes. (I, xvi, p.34–35)

The scene of the interrogation of Annie Weeks reveals that the Amer-Indians had taken her captive. Even though she is well treated by the Indian and kept like a privileged wife, Annie cannot see the Amer-Indian as human or an equal. There is evidence that the white woman held a great deal of power in the racialized space of Empire, and we see this in Annie's exertion of authority over Watanye: in one instance, at her behest, he spares the life of her captured father.[9] The relation here is complex between the strong (Europe) and the weak (the Amer-Indian) as it is played out in an inversion of the terms of power between the stereotypical man/woman. Authority and power are inversed and reversed in the construction of a discourse of white gender power which is able to assert itself in the territory of the 'savage'. There is no evidence of killings; only that the white girl Annie had been taken as an exclusive squaw which speaks of the native 'savage's fetishization of the European gendered Other. In this scene we see the agonistic relationship of the sexual attraction between the European white and the person of colour: both attract and repel each other.[10] In a discourse of power aided by moral superiority, the Ute Indians are clearly not regarded as human and the cohabitation of the European Annie with the Amer-Indian Watanye is seen as an affront to the propriety of the European. Again by the othering process the Indian's co-habitation with several squaws is seen as immoral, an excess of sexuality to the puritanical European. (Act II, pp.36ff) Said maintained that texts and discourses about the Orient not only defined the subaltern but edited him; 'he excised from it what [...] might have ruffled the European sensibility. In most cases the Orient seemed to have offended sexual propriety; everything about the Orient [...] exuded dangerous sex, threatened hygiene and domestic seemliness.'[11] 'Controlling women's sexuality, exalting maternity and breeding a virile race of empire builders were widely perceived as the paramount means for controlling the health and wealth of the imperial body politic [thus] sexual purity emerged as a controlling metaphor for racial, economic and political power.'[12] The anxiety around Annie's abduction is a European narrative of the construction of native degeneracy and white woman's 'rape'. It constructs Europe as morally superior by othering the native in a process which establishes a power constructed by obliterating and undermining the difference in which the native other is constructed. The othering is also an affect of the technology of Christian discourse: the native Other represents the hated vices personified so often in mediaeval church drama.

Act I, scene xi details the white man's treaty (pp. 24–25). Jean O'Brien speaks of the dispossession by degrees that the Indians experienced in the late eighteenth century, rendering them invisible as they creatively resisted colonialism by rebuilding kin networks and community outside their previously owned lands, which were seized by the British in a series of treaties that were not honoured. They lost control over the adjudication of land disputes, and collective ownership gave way to individual titles. Indian decision-making succumbed to English law and politics which made them invisible, enabling the construction of myth of Indian extinction. Although rendered invisible within the larger colonial social order, the Indian survived, and was not made extinct.[13] By the end of the century, O'Brien concludes, the English no longer cared about the cultural practices of the Amer-Indians: "They defined them as entirely extraneous to the social order".[14]

The end of the play sees the defeat of the Amer-Indians as they surrender: 'Once I moved like the wind. Now I surrender to you, and that is all.' (II, xxiii) The primarily white audience is addressed directly and implicated:

Indian:	You have driven us out. We have no more heart.
	I hate all white people.
	You have taken away all our lands. You have made us outcasts.
	You do not know how to share.
Squaw:	Blood to water, water to stone, stone to ash.
	Farewell, Crow country. (II, xxiii)

Depicting the civilized as savage further turns this play into a complex rendition of colonialism. Cannibalism, which stereotypically separated the civilized from the savage other of Europe in traditional colonial discourse is inverted by Gems. The idea of a superior morality which the colonizer used to justify his territorial conquest and rule was to a great extent derived from depicting the savage as cannibal as well as violent and unruly. Gems satirizes the European colonizer through so-called Christianity in America, among the lands of the natives as the colonizers of the new land worship the Lord in Act I, scene xiii, (p.26). Directly after the prayers, scene xiv sees Josiah Weeks make a beast of himself as he violently whips his wife as she struggles to go on with the trail. The Plains are harsh and the luxury he promised his wife they would travel in is nowhere to be seen. There is, in fact, a lot of suffering and hardship in the travel for territory and gold. Starvation, exhaustion, death of infants are common. It is here we see the European conquerors' cannibalism, greed, murder of loved ones in the struggle for food to survive. Anne McClintock explains the anti-social behaviour of the explorers by way of Victor Turner's concept of liminality:

Having sailed beyond the limits of their charted seas, explorers enter what Victor Turner calls a liminal condition. For Turner, a liminal condition is ambiguous, eluding 'the network of classifications that normally locate status and positions in cultural space'. There on the margins between known and unknown, the male conquistadors, explorers and sailors became creatures of transition and threshold [...] The men of margins were 'licensed to waylay, steal, rape. [...] To behave anti-socially is the proper expression of their marginal condition.'[15]

Gems' is a discourse of the politics of lust and violence that the imperialists are constituted in and governed by as they conquer new territories and acquire gold whilst indulging in cannibalism, eating their dead (II, xxiv, pp.57–58). Their material success is built upon greed, suffering and evil as they create their notion of 'civilisation'.

The 'discoverers' – filthy, ravenous, unhealthy and evil-smelling as they most likely were, scavenging along the edges of their known world and beaching on the fatal shores of their 'new' worlds, their limbs pocked with abcess and ulcers, their minds infested with fantasies of the unknown – had stepped far beyond any sanctioned guarantees. Their unsavoury rages, their massacres and rapes, their atrocious rituals of militarized masculinity sprang not only from the economic lust for spices, silver and gold, but also from the implacable rage of paranoia.[16]

This was the way the Europeans built civilization, this was the rage and lust it was founded on. The ambivalence on which colonial identity is constructed is laid bare in this play. It is Annie whose words, ironically celebratory but agonistically laden with irony for the audience and readers, close the play: '... *civilization ... We made it. We made it.*' From the perspective of this feminist play, or what Jonathan Gems calls 'a rite of passage drama in which a Victorian wife is transformed by the vicissitudes of the "great trek" into a modern woman',[17] western woman is revealed as partaking equally of the colonial construction of America.

Gems reinterprets East-West relations, rescuing them from the stereotype laid out in traditional colonial discourse (Frantz Fanon) or even seemingly radical books like Said's *Orientalism*. *Go West, Young Woman* is a harsh indictment of colonialism, and this early play neither excises nor edits in the manner of early European fiction writers but strives to present an honest and complex picture of the foundations of so-called civilization and culture by problematizing the relations and behaviours of the colonizer and the colonized. It is an essay in cultural resistance which subverts totalizing theories about American colonization.

Deborah's Daughter is set in an unnamed Islamic country in northern Africa (Egypt?) which is constructed like Said's Orient. Here, the setting is in contemporary time, the native educated in English and 'civilized'. Pederson Oil company's Deborah Pedersen, widow of the late Pedersen, is benefactress to this developing country. The play opens with a ceremony in which she presents a cheque of $20 million 'to make the desert flourish'. The wealth and generosity of the European benefactor constructs and others the attitude of the Islamic Other. The politics of transnational companies is played out here: Pedersen Oil is buying its way into the economy of this newly forming state. The power of the European Other is seen in the scene where Deborah Pedersen stops armed rebels from shooting. Although critics said that this scene betrayed naive writing,[18] it is in this scene that Gems most strongly plays off the difference between the power of the European and the impoverished desert state. 'The play is densely packed with the topical tangle of aid and trade, and the way we buy up bits of the Third World.'[19] And, indeed, this Third World state is dependent upon the Pedersen Oil for its sustenance. This dependency and a simultaneous need for self-sufficiency is what parallels the relationships Deborah Pederson has with the Islamic state as well as her daughter, Stephanie. The unnamed state, like Stephanie, needs to be independent and self-reliant, and that is the most potent message of this seemingly simply written piece.

Interestingly, the West here is woman (Deborah) while the East is male (Colonel Hassan Sa'id Ibn Sa'id). Hassan romanticizes and fetishizes the West in a paradox, as the West has done traditionally to the East as Said establishes in *Orientalism*.

> Hassan: Your soul is like the most beautiful flower ... shining ... fertile [...] I desire you. You are a sweet herb, a branch of fragrant rosemary. (II, ii)
> Hassan: And your hair, the colour of pale fire in the dark desert night – (II, v)

West and East in the play assume an inverse relationship: unlike Said's narration of the western construction of the Oriental in colonial discourse as childlike and the West as mature adult,[20] Deborah's fits and rages and petulance cast her in a role which is stereotypical of gender rather than geographical location. This makes the relationship between East and West rather more hierarchically complex than western Orientalists' or postcolonial scholars' analyses. It is the global capitalism of companies such as Pedersen Oil which finally determines the relationship between West and East: Europe is still strong to the East's impoverished and submissive Other despite the paradox of the individuals who are appointed to designate the two halves. The gender relationships in this play present a departure from the rigid stereotypes of Fanon's *Black Skin, White Masks*.[21] While Fanon's black man voices the need and desire to *be* white, the Middle-Eastern man of colour of the play exudes a confidence that Fanon's blacks are denied.

Pam Gems in these two plays demonstrates that white mythology can be contested from within the space of white writing:

> Metaphysics – the white mythology which reassembles and reflects the culture of the West: the *white man* takes his own mythology, Indo-European mythology, his own *logos*, that is, the *mythos* of his idiom, for the universal form of that he must still wish to call Reason. *Which does not go uncontested.*[22]

The two plays contest Said's theories of Orientalism and also Fanon's stereotypes of black and white relationships by making the inter-racial relationships more complex than merely a masculinized powerful West or a feminized passive East. The plays debunk colonial and postcolonial theorizing of colonial/colonized relationships as Gems establishes that white writing can create and represent the person of colour in new and complex ways. Gems does British drama a service by negotiating in her writing the circuitous impulses which make for eastern and western relationships demonstrating that neither man nor woman, West nor East can be dichotomized or stereotyped as easily as postcolonial and feminist scholars have maintained. That the relationships of gender, power and the Other are far more infinitely complex than are generally theorized is what her writing finally reveals.

Notes

1. Jean-Paul Sartre, *Being and Nothingness: An Essay in Phenomenological Ontology*, [1943] trans. Hazel E. Barnes, Methuen, 1958, p.222.
2. See Jean-Paul Sartre, *Being and Nothingness*, pp.302-303.
3. See Robert Ardrey who contends that territorial acquisition and defence is human 'open instinct'. *The Territorial Imperative*, Fontana, 1967.
4. http://www.washington.edu/alumni/columns/june95/asa_mercer.html.
5. See http://newman.baruch.cuny.edu/digital/2001/beecher/catherine.html.
6. Pam Gems, Foreword to *Go West, Young Woman*.
7. Edward W. Said, *Orientalism*, Vintage, 1979, p. 27.
8. See *Orientalism*, p.21.
9. See Anne McClintock, *Imperial Leather: Race, Gender and Sexuality in the Colonial Contest*, Routledge, 1995.
10. See Robert Young, *Colonial Desire: Hybridity in Theory, Culture and Race*, Routledge, 1995.
11. *Orientalism*, p.167.
12. *Imperial Leather*, p.47.

13. Jean O'Brien, *Dispossession by Degrees: Indian Land and Identity in Natick, Massachusetts, 1650–1790*, Cambridge University Press, 1997.

14. *Dispossession by Degrees*, p.198.

15. Anne McClintock, *Imperial Leather: Race, Gender and Sexuality in the Colonial Contest*, Routledge, 1995, pp.24-25. Quoting Victor Turner, *The Ritual Process: Structure and Anti-Structure*, Cornell University Press, 1969; Mary Douglas, *Purity and Danger*, Routledge and Kegan Paul, 1966.

16. *Imperial Leather*, p.28.

17. Letter to the author, 9 August 2002.

18. See Benedict Nightingale, *The Times*, 8 March 1994; John Peter, *Sunday Times*, 13 March 1994.

19. Robin Thorber, *The Guardian*, 7 March 1994.

20. 'The Oriental is irrational, depraved (fallen), childlike, "different"; […] the European is rational, virtuous, mature, "normal."' Edward Said, *Orientalism*, p.40.

21. See Frantz Fanon, *Black Skin, White Masks* [1952], trans. Charles Lam Markmann, Grove Press, 1967. Chapters 2 & 3.

22. Jacques Derrida, 'White Mythology' (1971), in *Margins of Philosophy*, trans. Alan Bass, Chicago: Chicago University Press, 1982, p.213. Emphases mine, except for the Greek words which are italicized in the original.

Conclusion

As far back as 1980, a theatre reviewer placed Gems' writing 'outside the feminist mode.'[1] The 1980s feminists were mostly separatist, had not yet theorized about nor included lesbian feminism and excluded racial others. Before these issues gripped feminism and asked of the movement to extend itself, Gems' plays were 'queer readings' of the stage in the best sense of the Sinfeldian term. The working-class, part-gypsy Pam Gems has, in the gamut of her writing, demonstrated the presence of class, race, gender and sexuality, bringing these issues into the heart of the British mainstream in plays that represent, question and entertain even as they destroy the centuries-old forms and styles of male dominated theatre. Her queer mythologizing brings into theatre the instructive fictionalizing of various categories which question the male tradition of white mythology which has denied identity space to the various others of malestream drama. Her bold, dramatic parts for women balanced always by her inclusion of men, combined with the non-linear quick filmic scenes make hers an innovative presence in the theatre. As a theatre-maker, Gems has broken much new ground which will serve as an example for future playwrights to emulate, making her one of the most influential playwrights of contemporary British drama.

Notes
1. Geraldine Pluenneke, *International Herald Tribune*, 28 May 1980.

BIBLIOGRAPHY

BOOKS AND ARTICLES

Acheson, James, ed., *British and Irish Drama since 1960*, The Macmillan Press, 1993.

Ardrey, Robert, *The Territorial Imperative*, Fontana, 1967.

Barthes, Roland, *Mythologies* [1957], trans. Jonathan Cape, 1972, Vintage, 1993.

Barthes, Roland, *The Pleasure of the Text* (*Le Plaisir du texte*, 1973) trans. Richard Miller, Farrar, Straus and Giroux, 1975.

Barthes, Roland, *Image - Music - Text*, Fontana Press, 1977.

Beauvoir, Simone de, *The Second Sex* (*Le Deuxième Sexe*, 1949), trans. and ed., H. M. Parshley, Jonathan Cape, 1953, reprt. Penguin 1983.

Benhabib, Seyla, and Cornell, Drucilla, eds., *Feminism As Critique*, Oxford University Press, 1987.

Benjamin, H., *The Transsexual Phenomenon*, Julian Press, 1966.

Berger, Maurice, Wallis, Brian and Watson, Simon, eds., *Constructing Masculinity*, Routledge, 1995.

Brater, Enoch, *Feminine Focus: The New Women Playwrights*, Oxford University Press, 1989.

Bristow, Joseph, *Effeminate England: Homoerotic Writing after 1885*, Columbia University Press, 1995.

Butler, Judith, *Gender Trouble: Feminism and the Subversion of Identity*, Routledge, 1990.

Butler, Judith, *Bodies That Matter: On the Discursive Limits of Sex*, Routledge, 1993.

Hart, Lynda, ed., *Making a Spectacle: Feminist Essays on Contemporary Theatre*, University of Michigan Press, 1989

Case, Sue-Ellen, *Feminist Theatre*, Macmillan, 1988.

Cixous, Hélène, 'The Laugh of the Medusa', in *New French Feminisms*, eds. Elaine Marks and Isabelle de Courtivron, Harvester, 1980.

Cixous, Hélène, and Clément, Catherine *The Newly Born Woman*, (*La Jeune Née*), pub. 1975, trans. Betsy Wing, University of Minnesota Press, 1986.

Cixous, Hélène, 'Aller à la mer' (1977), in Richard Drain (ed.), *Twentieth Century Theatre: A Sourcebook*, London and New York: Routledge, 1995.

Collis, Louise, *A Private View of Stanley Spencer*, William Heinemann Ltd, 1972.

Cotton, Nancy, *Woman Playwrights in England c.1363-1750*, New Jersey, London and Toronto: Associated University Presses, 1980.

Crisp, Quentin, *The Naked Civil Servant*, Plume, 1977.

Crosby, Christina, *The Ends of History: Victorians and 'The Woman Question'*, Routledge, 1991.

Deleuze, Gilles and Félix Guattari, *Anti-Oedipus: Capitalism and Schizophrenia Vol. I*, [*L'Anti-oedipe*, 1972], trans. Robert Hurley, Mark Seem, and Helen R. Lane, Athlone Press, 1984.

Derrida, Jacques, 'White Mythology' (1971), in *Margins – of Philosophy*, trans. Alan Bass, Chicago University Press, 1982.

Docter, Richard F., *Transvestites and Transsexuals: Toward a Theory of Cross-Gender Behaviour*, Plenium Press, 1988.

Douglas, Mary, *Purity and Danger*, Routledge and Kegan Paul, 1966.

Durant, Will, *The Story of Philosophy*, Washington Square Press, 1926. Reprt. 1953.

Elam, Diane, *Feminism and Deconstruction: Ms. en Abyme*, Routledge, 1994.

Fanon, Frantz (1967), *Black Skin, White Masks*, [*Peau Noire, Masques Blancs* 1952], trans. Charles Lam Markmann, Grove Press.

Ferris, Lesley, ed., *Crossing the Stage: Controversies on Cross Dressing*, Routledge, 1993.

Foucault, Michel, *Herculine Barbin: Being the Recently Discovered Memoirs of a Nineteenth-Century French Hermaphrodite*, [*Herculine Barbin, dite Alexina B.*], pub. Gallimard, 1978, trans. Richard McDougall, The Harvester Press, 1980.

Foucault, Michel, *Afterword, 'The Subject and Power'*, in Hubert Dreyfus and Paul Rabinow, *Michel Foucault: Beyond Structuralism and Hermeneutics*, University of Chicago Press, 1982.

Foucault, Michel, *The History of Sexuality Volume I*, [*La Volonté de savoir*, 1976], trans. Robert Hurley [1972], Penguin, 1990.

Garber, Marjorie, *Vice Versa: Bisexuality and the Eroticism of Everyday Life*, Hamish Hamilton, 1995.

Gardner, Lyn, 'Precious Gems', *Plays and Players*, April 1985.

Gems, Pam, 'Imagination and Gender', in *On Gender and Writing*, ed. Michelene Wandor, Pandora Press, 1983.

Gems, Pam, *After Birthday; My Warren; The Treat; Ladybird, Ladybird; Up in Sweden; Arthur and Guinevere; La Pasionaria; Blue Angel; Franz Into April; Garibaldi; Ebba; Go West, Young Woman, Aunt Mary*, unpublished manuscripts.

Gems, Pam, *Betty's Wonderful Christmas*, St Luke's Press, 1970.

Gems, Pam, *Queen Christina*, St Luke's Press, 1982.

Gems, Pam, *Dusa, Fish, Stas and Vi* in *Plays by Women: Vol. 1*, ed. Michelene Wandor, Methuen, 1983.

Gems, Pam, *Three Plays: Piaf / Camille / Loving Women*, Penguin, 1985.

Gems, Pam, *Stanley*, Nick Hern, 1997.

Gems, Pam, *Marlene*, Oberon, 1998.

Gems, Pam, *Deborah's Daughter*, Nick Hern, 1995.

Godiwala, Dimple, *Breaking the Bounds: British Feminist Dramatists Writing in the Mainstream since c. 1980*, Peter Lang, 2003.

Godiwala, Dimple and Haney II, William S., 'Editorial: Derrida's Indian Philosophical Subtext', *Consciousness, Literature and the Arts*, Volume 5, Number 2, August 2004. http://www.aber.ac.uk/tfts/journal [Archive].

Godiwala, Dimple, 'The Sacred and the Feminine: Indian women poets writing since 600 BCE', *LinQ*, forthcoming.

Griffiths, Trevor R., and Llewellyn-Jones, Margaret, ed., *British and Irish Women Dramatists since 1958*, Oxford University Press, 1993.

Hauser, Kitty, *Stanley Spencer*, Princeton University Press, 2001.

Holland, Eugene W., *Deleuze and Guattari's Anti-Oedipus: Introduction to Schizoanalysis*, Routledge, 1999.

Horrocks, Roger, *Masculinity in Crisis*, Macmillan, 1994.

Horrocks, Roger, *Male Myths and Icons: Masculininity in Popular Culture,* Macmillan, 1995.

Irigaray, Luce, 'This Sex which is not One'.

Kaplan, E. Ann, *Feminism and Film*, Oxford University Press, 2000.

Kauffman, L., ed., *American Feminist Thought at Century's End – A Reader*, Blackwell, 1993.

Lacan, Jacques, *Encore 1972-1973*, trans. Bruce Fink, Norton, 1998.

Landy, Marcia and Villarejo, Amy, *Queen Christina*, British Film Institute, 1995.

Macey, David, *Lacan in Contexts*, Verso, 1988.

MacInnes, John, *The End of Masculinity*, Open University Press, 1998.

MacKinnon, Kenneth, *Representing Men*, Arnold, 1993.

Marks, Elaine and Courtivron, Isabelle de, eds., *New French Feminisms* Harvester, 1980.

Marlowe, Kenneth, *The Male Homosexual*, Los Angeles: Medco, 1968.

McClintock, Anne, *Imperial Leather: Race, Gender and Sexuality in the Colonial Contest*, Routledge, 1995.

Millan, Betty, *Monstrous Regiment: Women Rulers in Men's Worlds*, The Kensal Press, 1982.

Norbrook, David, ed. *The Penguin Book of Renaissance Verse 1509–1659*, Penguin, 1992.

O'Brien, Jean, *Dispossession by Degrees: Indian Land and Identity in Natick, Massachusetts,*

1650–1790, Cambridge University Press, 1997.

Perls, Fritz, *Ego, Hunger and Aggression*, Random House, 1969.

Pople, Kenneth, *Stanley Spencer: A Biography*, William Collins, 1991.

Prosser, Jay, 'Transgender' in Andy Medhurst and Sally R. Munt (eds.), *Lesbian and Gay Studies: A Critical Introduction*, Cassell, 1997.

Remnant, Mary, ed., *Plays by Women: Volume Five*, Methuen, 1986.

Rich, Adrienne, *Of Woman Born: Motherhood as Experience and Institution*, first published, USA: 1976; UK Virago 1977.

Said, Edward W., *Orientalism*, Vintage, 1979.

Sandford, Stella, 'Contingent Ontologies: Sex, gender and 'woman' in Simone de Beauvoir and Judith Butler', *Radical Philosophy*, No.97, September/October 1999.

Sartre, Jean-Paul, *Being and Nothingness: An Essay in Phenomenological Ontology*, [1943] trans. Hazel E. Barnes, Methuen, 1958.

Scolnicov, Hanna, and Holland, Peter, *The Play out of Context: Transferring Plays from Culture to Culture*, eds. Cambridge University Press, 1989.

Senelick, Laurence, *The Changing Room: Sex, Drag and Theatre*, Routledge, 2000.

Sinfield, Alan, 'Transgender and les/bi/gay identities' in David Alderson and Linda Anderson (eds.), *Territories of Desire in Queer Culture: Reconfiguring contemporary boundaries*, Manchester University Press, 2000.

Sinfield, Alan, *Cultural Politics: Queer Reading*, University of Pennsylvania Press, 1994.

Sinfield, Alan, *The Wilde Century: Effeminacy, Oscar Wilde and the Queer Moment*, Columbia University Press, 1994.

Stephenson, Heidi, and Langridge, Natasha, *Rage and Reason: Women Playwrights on Playwriting*, Methuen, 1997.

Turner, Victor, *The Ritual Process: Structure and Anti-Structure*, Cornell University Press, 1969

Wandor, Michelene, ed., *On Gender and Writing*, Pandora Press, 1983.

Wandor, Michelene, *Carry On, Understudies*, Routledge and Kegan Paul, 1981, reprt.1986

Wandor, Michelene, *Plays by Women: Volume I*, Methuen, 1983

Wilcox, Timothy, ed., *The Art of Hilda Carline, Mrs. Stanley Spencer*, Lincolnshire County Council, the Usher Gallery, 1999.

Williams, Tennessee, *Penguin Plays: Sweet Bird of Youth / A Streetcar Named Desire / The Glass Menagerie*, Penguin Books, 1959.

Young, Robert, *Colonial Desire: Hybridity in Theory, Culture and Race*, Routledge, 1995.

NEWSPAPERS

Pauline Peters in *The Sunday Times*, 3 February 1980.

Geraldine Pluenneke, *International Herald Tribune*, 28 May 1980.

John Barber in *The Daily Telegraph*, 2 February 1984.
Michael Ratcliffe in *The Observer*, 5 February 1984.
Michael Billington in *The Guardian*, 15 December 1993.
Jack Tinker, *The Daily Mail*, 14 December 1993.
Benedict Nightingale in *The Times*, 15 December 1993.
Louise Doughty in *The Mail on Sunday*, 19 December 1993.
Irving Wardle in *The Independent*, 19 December 1993.
Benedict Nightingale in *The Times*, 15 December 1993.
Charles Spencer in *The Daily Telegraph*, 15 December 1993.
Clive Hirschhorn in *Sunday Express*, 19 December 1993.
Sheridan Morley in *The Spectator*, 1 January 1994.
Robin Thorber, *The Guardian*, 7 March 1994.
Benedict Nightingale, *The Times*, 8 March 1994
John Peter, *Sunday Times*, 13 March 1994.
Robert Fulford, *The National Post*, 23 October 2001.

INTERVIEWS
Pam Gems in *Spare Rib*, September 1977
Pam Gems in an interview with the author, 8 May 2001.
Pam Gems in an interview with Jonathan Gems, April 2004. Documented in a letter
    from Jonathan Gems to the author, 18 April 2004.

CORRESPONDENCE
Letter to the author from Pam Gems, 8 November 2000.
Letter to the author from Jonathan Gems, 9 August 2002.
Letter to the author from Jonathan Gems, 18 April 2004.

CDs
Legends of the Twentieth Century: Edith Piaf, EMI CD.

WEBSITES
*Note: The author takes no responsibility for the malfunctioning or eventual
disappearance of the websites listed. At the time of writing these sites were
functioning and available.*

Chastain, James, compiler: http://www.ohiou.edu/~chastain/dh/gari.htm.
    Cecchini, Ezio. "Le Campagne di Garibaldi. 1849." *Rivista Militare* 105 (1982,
    n.2), 197–205; Coppa, Frank J. *The Origins of the Italian Wars of Independence.*
    London and New York: Longman, 1992; Garibaldi, Giuseppe. *Autobiography*, trans.

A Werner. New York: Howard Fertig, 1971; Garibaldi, Giuseppe. *Memoire*, ed. Ugoberto Alfessio Grimaldi. Verona: Bertani editore, 1972; Ridley, Joseph. *Garibaldi*. New York: Viking, 1976; Trevelyan, George Macaulay. *Garibaldi and the Thousand*. New York: Longman, 1948; Ugolini, Romano. *Garibaldi. Genesi di un mito*. Rome: Ateneo, 1982.

Gems, Keith, http://www.ucl.ac.uk/~ucbtdag/bioethics/Keith.html and http://www.geocities.com/FashionAvenue/1122/mannequin_gallery/gemini/

Godiwala, Dimple and Haney II, William S., 'Editorial: Derrida's Indian Philosophical Subtext', *Consciousness, Literature and the Arts*, Volume 5, Number 2, August 2004. http://www.aber.ac.uk/tfts/journal [Archive]

Wertheimer, Max, lecture on Gestalt theory, 1924, http://www.enabling.org/ia/gestalt/gerhards/wert1.html

http://www.washington.edu/alumni/columns/june95/asa_mercer.html

http://newman.baruch.cuny.edu/digital/2001/beecher/catherine.html

APPENDIX
(COMPILED BY JONATHAN GEMS)

Aunt Mary (1982)
The Cherry Orchard (adaptation) (1984)
Loving Women (1984)
Camille (adaptation) (1984)
Pasionaria (1985)
The Danton Affair (adaptation) (1986)
The Blue Angel (adaptation) (1988)
Arthur and Guinevere (1990)
The Seagull (adaptation) (1991)
Deborah's Daughter (1992)
Ghosts (adaptation) (1994)
Stanley (1996)
Marlene (1996)
At The Window (1997)
The Snow Palace (1998)
Ebba (1999)

The Late Plays (2000–)
Garibaldi, Si! (2000)
Linderhof (2001)
Mrs Pat (2002)
Yerma (adaptation) (2003)
Not Joan The Musical (2003)
The Lady From The Sea (adaptation) (2003)
Cheri (adaptation) (2003)
The Little Mermaid (adaptation) (2004)
Nelson (2004)

Other Works:
A Builder By Trade (TV Play) (1962)
The Russian Princess (TV Play) (1966)
Mrs Frampton (novel) (1989)
Bon Voyage, Mrs Frampton (novel) (1990)
Stanley's Women (screenplay) (1999)
Finchie's War (screenplay) (2001)

PRODUCTION INFORMATION
Betty's Wonderful Christmas (1972)
The Amiable Courtship of Miz Venus And Wild Bill (1973)
First performed at the Almost Free Theatre, Camden, London, on 29th October, 1973.
Produced by Ed Berman and Inter-Action.

Go West Young Woman (1974)
First performed at the Roundhouse, Camden, London, on 11th June 1974. Produced by the Women's Company – with the following cast:

Stuart Barren
Kate Beswick
Helen Downing
Ron Forfar
Jonina Scott
Ellen Sheen
Malcolm Bullivant
Margie Campi
Patricia Franklin
Thea Ranft
Don Warrington

Directed by	Susan Todd with Ann Mitchell
Designed by	Sarah Paulley
Musical Director	Bobby Campbell
Accompaniment	Tom Paley
Production Assistant	Buzz Goodbody
Voice Consultant	Bettina Jonic
Stage Management	Sarah Gems and Claire Higney

Up In Sweden (1975)
First performed at the Haymarket Studio, Leicester, in 1975.

My Name Is Rosa Luxembourg (1976)
Version by Pam Gems of the play by Mariane Auricoste.
First performed at the Soho Poly in 1976.

Rivers And Forests (1976)

Version by Pam Gems of the play Marguerite Duras.
First performed at the Soho Poly in 1976.

Dusa, Fish, Stas and Vi (1976)

First produced at the Hampstead Theatre on 8th December 1976; subsequently presented by Michael Codron at the Mayfair Theatre on 10th February 1977 with the following cast:

DUSA ....Brigit Forsyth
FISH ....Alison Fiske
STAS ....Diane Fletcher
VIOLET ....Mary Maddox

Directed by ....Nancy Meckler
Designed by...Tanya McCallin

Alison Fiske won The Laurence Olivier Award for Best Actress.

Franz Into April (1977)

First performed at the Institute Of Contemporary Arts in 1977.

FRANZ ....Warren Mitchell

Queen Christina (1977)

First Produced by the Royal Shakespeare Company at The Other Place, Stratford-upon-Avon, in Ocotber 1977. The cast was as follows:

QUEEN CHRISTINA...Sheila Allen
CHRISTINA AS A CHILD ....Erin Tyler
CHANCELLOR AXEL OXENSTIERNA ....Bernard Brown
KING GUSTAVUS ADOLPHUS.........................Barry Rutter
GERMAN PRINCE ....Iain Mitchell
GERMAN AMBASSADOR ....John Burgess
LADY EBBA SPARRE ....Charlotte Cornwall
QUEEN MOTHER ....Valerie Lush
DESCARTES ....John Burgess
MAGNUS DE LA GUARDIE ....Nigel Terry
PRINCE KARL ....Ian McNeice

GIRL ....Fleur Chandler
CHANUT ....Barry Rutter
SECRETARY ....Ian Mitchell
COPLEMAN ....Nigel Terry
DUKE ....Ian Mitchell
BISHOP ....John Burgess
MARQUISE ....Valerie Lush
MARIANNE ....Fleur Chandler
CATHERINE DE ROHANT ....Charlotte Cornwall
COUNT DE BREVAYE ....Iain Mitchell
POPE ....Bernard Brown
MONALDESCHO ....Nigel Terry
CARDINAL AZZOLINO ....Ian McNeice
CAPTAIN ....John Burgess
SOLDIER ....Barry Rutter
LUCIA..Valerie Rush
ANGELICA AS A CHILD ....Erin Tyler
ANFELICA ....Fleur Chandler
RUFFINO..Ian Mitchell
ROMANO ....Barry Rutter
SALVATORE ....Nigel Terry
MUSICIAN ....Robin Weatherall

Directed by ....Penny Cherns
Designed by..Di Seymour
Music by..Guy Woolfendon
Lighting by ....Leo Leibovici
Choreography by ....Gillian Lynne
Fight directed by.......................................Nick Stranger
Company Voice work by ....Cicely Berry
Administrator of The Other Place ....Ron Daniels

Piaf (1978)

First presented at the Other Place, Stratford-upon-Avon, by the Royal Shakespeare Company on 5th October 1978. Subsequently at the Aldwych and Piccadilly Theatres. The cast was as follows:

PAIF ....Jane Lapotaire
TOINE ....Zoe Wanamaker

MARLENE ....Darlene Johnson
MADELEINE...Carmen du Sautoy
NURSE ....Susanna Bishop
INSPECTOR/ BARMAN and GEORGES ....Conrad Asquith
LOUIS/ BUTCHER/ DOPE PUSHER and LUCIEN ....Bill Buffery
MAN AT REHEARSAL and PIERRE.....................Ian Charleson
MANAGER ....Geoffrey Freshwater
LOUIS 'PAPA' LEPLÉE and JEAN ....James Griffiths
EMIL/JACKO and EDDIE................................Allan Hendrick
ANGELO and GERMAN SOLDIER ....Anthony Higgins
PAUL/ AMERICAN SAILOR and PHYSIOTHERAPIST ....Ian Reddington
LEGIONNAIRE/ JACQUES/ GERMAN SOLDIER/
MARCEL/ AMERICAN SOLDIER and THEO ....Malcolm Storry
MUSIC DIRECTOR/ PIANO ....Michael Tubs
ACCORDIAN ....Roy Stelling

Directed by ....Howard Davies
Designed by...Douglas Heap

Jane Lapotaire won the Society of West End Theatres Award for Best Actress.

Other productions include:
The Playhouse, Melbourne, Australia (13th May–27th June) produced by the
    Melbourne Theatre Company, starring Caroline O'Connor.
The Stadsteatern, Stockholm, Sweden, starring Helen Bergstrom.
Thorndike Theatre and West End, London, starring Elaine Paige, directed by Peter
    Hall (1993).
Teatru Polskiego, Poland, starring Agnieszka Matysiak, directed by Jerzy Zagorski.
Kamaraszinhaz, Budapest, Hungary, starring Vari Eva (1995).
Thater am Kurfurstendamm, Berlin, Germany, starring Madeleine Lienhard (1995).
Mojo Theatre, Amsterdam, Holland, 1999, starring Liesbeth List, directed by Andy
    Daal.

Ladybird, Ladybird (1979)
First performed at the King's Head Theatre, 1979.

Aunt Mary (1982)

First produced at the Warehouse Theatre, London, on 15th June 1982 with the following cast:

MURIEL ....Ann Way
MARTIN ....Timothy Spall
MARY ....Charlie Paton
CYST ....Barry Jackson
JACK..Peter Attard
ALISON ....Patricia Quinn

Directed by ....Robert Walker
Designed by..David Fielding
Lighting by ....Charlie Paton
Stage managed by ....David Proctor
Deputy stage managed by ....Charlotte Warner
Assistant stage managed by............................Peter Stone

Camille (1984)

Based on *La Dame aux Camélias* by Alexandre Dumas *fils*.

First produced by the Royal Shakespeare Company at The Other Place, Stratford-upon-Avon, on April 4th 1984 with the following cast:

MARGUERITE GAULTIER ....Frances Barber
ARMAND DUVAL ....Nicholas Ferrell
PRUDENCE ....Polly James
SOPHIE ....Alphonsia Emmanuel
CLÉMENCE ....Rowena Roberts
JANINE/ OLYMPE...Katherine Rogers
YVETTE ....Sarah Woodward
GASTON DU MAURIEUX ....Paul Gregory
LE DUC..Norman Henry
COUNT DRUFTHEIM ....Charles Millham
M. DE SANCERRE ....Arthur Kohn
PRICE BELA MIRKASSIAN...............................Andrew Hall
JEAN...Peter Theedom
UPHOLSTERER ....Andrew Jarvis

ARMAND'S FATHER, THE MARQUIS DE
SAINT-BRIEUC...Bernard Horsfall
RUSSIAN PRINCE (SERGEI) ....Arthur Kohn

Other parts were played by members of the company. The pianist was James Walker.

Directed by ....Ron Daniels
Designed by..Maria Bjornson
Lighting by ....John Waterhouse
Music by...Guy Woolfenden
Choreography by ....Anthony van Laast
Fights arranged by ....Malcolm Ransom
Stage managed by ....Richard Oriel

Loving Women (1984)

First produced at the Arts Theatre, London, on 31st January 1984 by David Jones and Jonathan Gems with the following cast:

SUSANNAH ....Marion Bailey
FRANK ....David Beames
CRYSTAL ....Gwyneth Strong

Directed by ....Phillip Davis
Designed by..Jonathan Gems
Lighting by ....Stephen Rolfe
Production manager...Tony Harpur
Stage manager ....Evelyn Doggart
Costumes ....Kate Burnett
ASM ....Christine Harmar Brown
ASM ....Sarah Webster
Design Assistant ....Maggie Binoux

Other productions include: Palais Des Beaux-Arts, Brussels, Belgium, 1984, starring Anne Chappuis, Marie-Line Lefebvre and Jules-Henri Marchant, translated by Denyse Periez, directed by Adrian Brine.

Etcetera Theatre, Camden, London, starring Elizabeth Lewendon, Helena Lymbery, Alistair McGowan, directed by Tony Yates.

Pasionaria (1985)

First produced by the Tynewear Theatre Company at the Newcastle Playhouse on 12th February, 1985, with the following cast:

LA PASIONARIA (DOLORES IBARRURI) ....Denise Black
SENOR LOPEZ – UNION MAN –
   MANUEL SOLDIER – MAYOR –
   PRIME MINISTER ....Richard Albrecht
MINE MANAGER – PRISON GOVERNOR LUIS –
   PRISONER – FERNANDEZ...........................Richard Cordery
DOLORES'S FATHER – MINER – JESUS ....Shay Gorman
DOLORES'S HUSBAND – PEDLAR ....Daniel Hill
EMILIA – SENORA LOPEZ – WOMAN
   GOVERNOR – PRISONER ....Judy Hopton
DONA SEBASTIANA – PILAR – DANCER –
   CAFÉ SINGER – SECRETARY – DEPUTY ....Kate McKenzie
BONIFACIO'S MOTHER – JUANITA –
   MANUELA – PRISONER – MONTALBAN ....Mary Sheen
BONIFACIO – JOSE – SOLDIER – CIVIL
   GUARD – DEPUTY....................................Lucien Taylor

La Pasionaria's children played by Barbara and Stephen Hoare or Emma and James Taylor.

PERCUSSION ....Bruce Arthur
REEDS ....Francis Christou
GUITAR..Chris Glassfield

Choreography by Sue Dunderdale, Kate McKenzie, Josie Lawrence and Maria Emerson.

Directed by ....Sue Dunderdale
Designed by..Alexandra Byrne
Musical Director ....Paul Sand
Lighting byRoy Rennie

The Danton Affair (1986)

First performed at the Barbican Theatre, London, on July 15th 1986. Produced by The Royal Shakespeare Company, with the following cast:

DANTON...Brian Cox
ROBESPIERRE ....Ian McDiarmid

The Blue Angel (1991)
Based on the novel by Heinrich Mann.

First performed at the Other Place, Stratford-upon-Avon, 7th August 1991. Opened at The Globe Theatre, London, 20th May 1992. Produced by The Royal Shakespeare Company with the following cast:

LOLA ....Kelly Hunter
PROFESSOR RAAT ....Philip Madoc
MAI BOMBLER ....Judith Bruce
FRIEDRICH BOMBLER ....Sidney Livingstone
DIETER ....Peter-Hugo Daly
TUMTUM ....Cheryl Fergison
BERTHA ....Sarah Flind
KLAUS ....Julian Forsyth
COBBLER / DUTCH CAPTAIN / JANITOR /
     DR LIPPMANN / JUDGE ....Desmond McNamara
PAUL ....Patrick Toomey
HERMINE ....Jackie Ekers
HANS / HERR PRESSMAN ....Charles Simpson
LUTZ / WAITER / POLICEMAN......................Jonathan Weir
FRAU PFLUG / WAITRESS / HANNALESE /
     COBBLER'S WIFE / HAT-CHECK GIRL ....Arhlene Allan
HEADMASTER / POLICEMAN / MAYOR...........Allan Mitchell

Directed by ....Trevor Nunn
Designed by...Maria Bjornson
Choreography by ....David Toguri
Assistant Director ....William James
Musical Director..Steven Edis
Lighting by ....Chris Parry
Sound by ....Steven Brown
Wardrobe ....Allan Watkins
Production Manager ....Caro Mackay
Stage Manager ....Donna Wiffen

Produced by ....Mark Furness
....John Newman

Winner 'Best Entertainment' – Laurence Olivier Awards 1993.
Winner 'Best Actress' for Kell Hunter – Laurence Olivier Awards 1993.

Marlene (1996)
First presented at the Oldham Coliseum Theatre on 2nd October 1996 with the
following cast:

MARLENE ....Siân Phillips
VIVIAN HOFFMAN ....Lou Gish
MUTTI ....Billy Mathias

Piano..Kevin Amos
Violin ....Julian Jackson

Subsequently presented at the Lyric Theatre, Shaftesbury Avenue, London, on 8th
April 1997 with the addition of John Richards on Double Bass.

Directed by ....Sean Mathias
Musical direction by...Kevin Amos
Assistant direction by ....Thierry Harcourt
Designed by...Michael Vale
Clothes by...Terry Parsons
Lighting by ....Mark Jonathan
Sound by ....Clement Rawling

Winner 'Best Entertainment' – The Laurence Olivier Awards 1998.

Published by Oberon Books
521 Caledonian Road
London
N7 9RH
Tel: 020 7607/ Fax: 020 7607 3629
Email: oberon.books@btinternet.com
www.oberonbooks.com

Stanley (1996)

First staged by the National Theatre at the Cattesloe on 1st February 1996, with the following cast:

HILDA CARLINE ....Deborah Findlay
STANLEY SPENCER ....Anthony Sher
HENRY ....Pip Torrens
GWEN ....Nicola King
PATRICIA PREECE...Anna Chancellor
AUGUSTUS JOHN ....David Collings
DOROTHY...Selina Cadell
DUDLEY TOOTH ....Richard Howard
ELSIE ....Stephanie Jacob
MRS CARLINE ....Avril Elgar
BRIAN..Nicholas Deigman/
 ....Daniel Forster-Smith
TIM ....Robbie Morton/
 ....Robert Smythson

Other parts played by members of the Company.

Pianist/ keyboards...Walter Fabeck
Directed by ....John Caird
Designed by...Tim Hatley
Lighting by ....Peter Mumford
Company Voice Work by ....Patsy Rodenburg
Dialect Coach ....Jeanette Nelson
Sound ....Freya Edwards

Winner of the 1997 Laurence Olivier Award for 'Best Play'.
Anthony Sher won the 1997 Laurence Olivier Award for 'Best Actor'.
Deborah Findlay won the 1997 Laurence Olivier Award for 'Best Supporting Actress'

Production transferred to The Circle In The Square Theatre, Manhattan, New York, USA.

The Snow Palace (1998)

First performed at the Wilde Theatre, Bracknell on 22nd January 1998 and then toured with the following cast:

ST JUST ....Justin Avoth
MOTHER / AUNT HELENA / WOMAN ....Kristin Milward
STANISLAWA ....Kathryn Pogson
ROBESPIERRE ....Kenn Sabberton
ANNA / LOUISE ....Jemma Shaw
DANTON / FATHER ....Robert Wilcox

The London premiere was at the Tricycle Theatre on 1st December 1998 with the following cast:

ST JUST ....Justin Avoth
MOTHER / AUNT HELENA / WOMAN ....Kristin Milward
STANISLAWA ....Kathryn Pogson
ROBESPIERRE ....Nigel Cooke
ANNA / LOUISE ....Katrina Syran
DANTON / FATHER ....Mark Lewis Jones

Directed by ....Janet Suzman
Designed by...Bruce Macadie
Sound by ....John A. Leonard for Aura
Lighting by ....Ian Scott

Produced by The Sphinx Theatre Company.
Administrator: Sue Parrish.

Published by Oberon Books
521 Caledonian Road
London
N7 9RH
Tel: 020 7607/ Fax: 020 7607 3629
Email: oberon.books@btinternet.com
www.oberonbooks.com

Mrs Pat (2004)

First performed at RADA on 16th January 2004 with the following cast:

MRS PAT ....Celia Imrie

Other parts played by ....Hugh Fraser
....Richard Lintern
....Claudia Harrison
....James Topping

Directed by ....Sue Dunderdale

Deborah's Daughter (radio play)

First broadcast on BBC Radio 4 on 30th November 1992.
The cast included:

Prunella Scales
Raad Rawi
Elizabeth Spriggs
Keith Drinkel
Federay Holmes
Julian Rhind Tutt

Directed by ....Sue Dunderdale
Produced by ....Claire Grove

ENGLISH VERSIONS OF FOREIGN PLAYS

Uncle Vanya

By Anton Chekhov,
in a version by Pam Gems.

First performed at the Hampstead Theatre Club on 22 November 1979 with the following cast:

MARINA ....Hilda Braid
MICHAIL LYOVICH ASTROV ....Ian Holm
IVAN PETROVICH VOYNITSKY (Uncle Vanya) ......Nigel Hawthorne
ALEKSANDR VLADIMIROVICH SEREBRYAKOV ..Maurice Denham

YELENA ANDREYEVNA ....Susan Littler
SOFYA ALEKSANDROVNA (Sonya) ....Alison Steadman
ILYA ILYICH TELYEGIN (Waffle) ....Anthony O'Donnell
MARYA VASSILEYEVNA ....Jean Anderson
A WORKMAN...Peter Barnes

Directed by ....Nancy Meckler
Designed by...Alison Chitty
Costumes ....Lindy Hemming
Lighting ....Mark Jonathan
Company Manager ....Ruth Hogarth
Russian Consultant ....Tanya Alexander

Also staged at the National Theatre (Lyttelton) – first performance 18th May 1982 –
with the following cast:

MARINA ....Madoline Thomas
MICHAIL LYOVICH ASTROV ....Dinsdale Landen
IVAN PETROVICH VOYNITSKY (Uncle Vanya) ......Michael Bryant
ALEKSANDR VLADIMIROVICH SEREBRYAKOV ..Basil Henson
YELENA ANDREYEVNA ....Cherie Lunghi
SOFYA ALEKSANDROVNA (Sonya) ....Patti Love
ILYA ILYICH TELYEGIN (Waffle) ....Daniel Thorndyke
MARYA VASSILEYEVNA ....Madeleine Christie
A WORKMAN...Michel Beint

Directed by ....Michael Bogdanov
Designed by...John Bury
Lighting by ....Chris Ellis

Also staged at the Riverside Theatre, produced by the Renaissance Theatre Company
in 1990 – with the following cast:

MARINA ....Stella Moray
MICHAIL LYOVICH ASTROV ....Peter Egan
IVAN PETROVICH VOYNITSKY (Uncle Vanya) ......Richard Briars
ALEKSANDR VLADIMIROVICH SEREBRYAKOV ..Patrick Godfrey
YELENA ANDREYEVNA ....Sian Thomas
SOFYA ALEKSANDROVNA (Sonya) ....Annabel Arden

ILYA ILYICH TELYEGIN (Waffle) ....Jimmy Yuill
MARYA VASSILEYEVNA ....Olga Lowe
A WORKMAN..Alex Lowe
MAID ....Helen Goldwyn
WATCHMAN ....Robin Lloyd

Directed by ....Kenneth Branagh
Designed by...Kenny Miller
Lighting by ....Rick Fisher
Co-director ....Peter Egan
Costumes ....Susan Coates
Wardrobe ....Stephanie Collie
Production consultant ....Hugh Cruttwell
Production Manager ....Felix Davis
Stage Manager ....Christine Hathaway
Company Manager ....Chris Pickles
Producer ....David Parfitt

Also staged at the National Theatre (Cottesloe) – first performance 25th February 1992, with the following cast:

MARINA ....Antonia Pemberton
MICHAIL LYOVICH ASTROV ....Antony Sher
IVAN PETROVICH VOYNITSKY (Uncle Vanya) ......Ian McKellen
ALEKSANDR VLADIMIROVICH SEREBRYAKOV ..Eric Porter
YELENA ANDREYEVNA ....Janet McTeer
SOFYA ALEKSANDROVNA (Sonya) ....Lesley Sharp
ILYA ILYICH TELYEGIN (Waffle) ....Karl Johnson
MARYA VASSILEYEVNA ....Rachel Gurney
YEFIM...Barry Stearn
A WORKMAN..Paul McGrane

Directed by ....Sean Mathias
Designed by...Stephen Brimson Lewis
Lighting by ....Ben Ormerod

Produced by the Royal National Theatre.
Administrator ....Sir Richard Eyre

Published by Nick Hern Books
20 Vauxhall Bridge Road
London
SW1V 2SA

Janet McTeer won The Laurence Olivier Award for 'Best Actress'.

The Cherry Orchard
By Anton Chekhov

First performed on the Olivier stage of the National Theatre on 1st July 1994. The cast was as follows:

IRINA NIKOLAYEVNA ARKADINA ....Judi Dench
KONSTANTIN GAVRILOVICH TREPLEV ....Alan Cox
PYOTR NIKOLAYEVICH SORIN ....Norman Rodway
NINA MIKHAILOVNA ZARECHNAYA ....Helen McCrory
ILYA AFANASYEVICH SHAMRAYEV ....Robert Demeger
POLINA ANDREYEVNA ....Anna Calder-Marshall
MARYA ILYINICHNA – MASHA ....Rachel Power
BORIS ALEKSEYEVICH TRIGORIN ....Bill Nighy
YEVGENY SERGEYEVICH DORIN ....Edward Petherbridge
SEMYON SEMYONOVICH MEDVEDENKO ....John Hodgkinson
YAKOV ....Jimmy Gardner
A COOK ....John Muirhead
A MAID ....Penny Ryder

Musicians: ....Melanie Bush (clarinet/flute),
David Harrod (piano)

Directed by ....John Caird
Settings by ....John Gunter
Costumes by ....Fotini Dimou
Lighting by ....David Hersey
Music by ....Dominic Muldowney
Company voice work by ....Patsy Rodenburg
Literal translation by ....Helen Molchanoff

The Lady From The Sea
By Henrik Ibsen,
in a version by Pam Gems.

First performed at the Almeida Theatre, London, on 8th May 2003 with the following cast:

WANGEL ....John Bowe
ELLIDA ....Natasha Richardson
BOLETTE ....Claudia Blakely
HILDE...Louis Clein
ARNHOLM ....Tim McInnerny
LYNGSTRAND ....Benedict Cumberbatch
BALLESTED ....Geoffrey Hutchings
STRANGER ....Eoin McCarthy

Directed by ....Trevor Nunn
Designed by...Rob Howell
Lighting by ....Hugh Vanstone
Music ....Shaun Davey
Sound ....John Leonard

Produced by the Almeida Theatre Company.
Administrator: ....Michael Attenborough

Published by Oberon Books.
521 Caledonian Road
London
N7 9RH
Tel: 020 7607/ Fax: 020 7607 3629
Email: Oberon.books@btinternet.com
www.oberonbooks.com

Yerma
By Federico Garcia Lorca
in a version by Pam Gems.

First performed at the Royal Exchange Theatre, Manchester, on 22 January 2003, with the following cast:

YERMA ....Denise Black
JUAN ....Peter Gowen
MARIA ....Caoimhe Harvey
VICTOR ....Oliver Haden
PAGAN WOMAN ....Anni Domingo
DOLORES ....Eileen O'Brien
CONCHITA (FIRST YOUNG GIRL) ....Helen Kay
LOUISA (SECOND YOUNG GIRL)/
   MASKED DANCER ....Lydia Baksh
WOMAN ONE ....Orla Cottingham
WOMAN TWO ....Catriona Martin
WOMAN THREE ....Daniella Dessa
FIRST SISTER ....Laura Richmond
SECOND SISTER ....Jill Myers
SHEPHERD/MASKED DANCER ....Darren Mercer
MUSICIAN ....Akintayo Akinbode

Directed by ....Helena Kaut-Howson
Designed by..Simon Higlett
Music by..Akintayo Akinbode
Lighting by ....Jason Taylor

Published by Oberon Books
521 Caledonian Road
London
N7 9RH
Tel: 020 7607/ Fax: 020 7607 3629
Email: Oberon.books@btinternet.com
www.oberonbooks.com